THE 7 CORE SKILLS OF EVERYDAY HAPPINESS

Scientifically Proven Skills for a Happier, More Meaningful Life

SCOTT WILHITE

BOOKS™

For information about special discounts for bulk purchases, please contact:
sales@nCOURAGE.LIFE

Cover design: Scott Wilhite
Edited by: Ken Darrow
Interior design: Scott Wilhite

An imprint of Whispering Voice Books

Library of Congress Control Number: 2016918905
ISBN 0-9720760-1-8

The 7 Core Skills of Everyday Happiness: Scientifically Proven Skills for a Happier, More Meaningful Life / Wilhite, Scott, author / First edition

Give feedback on the book or share your success story at: results@nCOURAGE.LIFE

For additional positive mindset conditioning tools visit:
http://www.nCOURAGE.LIFE

To the destitute people of Cambodia
for inspiring me to seek for the
true wealth you clearly
already possess

PRAISE

Once you learn happiness is a skill, you'll never go back to just wishing for it.
— **Greg Reid**, best selling author, speaker, filmmaker

This book will teach you how to be as happy as the most naturally optimistic people you admire.
— **Shawn Achor**, New York Times best selling author of *The Happiness Advantage*

Learn the core skills that make life worth living.
— **Richie Norton**, best selling author of *The Power of Starting Something Stupid*

Forget motivational hoo-hah and get measurable results with Scott Wilhite's *The 7 Core Skills of Everyday Happiness*. Grounded in research, this book provides the science and tools to take charge of your happiness so you can live a life of abundance every single day.
— **Wendy Lipton-Dibner**, M.A., President, Professional Impact, Inc. and bestselling author of *Focus On Impact*® - The 10-Step Map to Reach Millions, Make Millions and Love Your Life Along the Way.

What sets this book apart is it doesn't simply promise a better life, it suggests specific valuable techniques to feel more cheerful in challenging times.
— **Ken Darrow**, M.A., 14x author, entrepreneur

CONTENTS

INTRODUCTION

THE CAMBODIAN SURPRISE

JULY 30, 2005. SOMEWHERE OUTSIDE OF PHNOM PENH, CAMBODIA. I was squished inside a rickety grey minivan between boxes of camera gear and members of the film crew. We were travelling down a poorly paved road to the southern province of Kampot near the Vietnam boarder. The air was hot and muggy. Because of the sensitivity of the camera, we couldn't run the air conditioner and instead had to drive with the windows rolled down. I grumbled as I noticed how my shirt was already soaked in sweat.

We had been sent to Cambodia to create a series of documentary films for a humanitarian group. The goal was to film sad, destitute people in order to instill empathy in a rich American audience and generate additional funding. As I glanced out the window I recognized we had one major problem—I didn't see a lot of unhappy people.

I saw uncomfortable people. I saw a family of five riding on a single motorcycle through crowded busy city streets. I saw penniless children dressed in rags sitting by the side of the road on dirty plastic barrels serving as makeshift chairs. And I saw dignified shopkeepers sweeping the top layer of dirt from the dirt road in front of their shop. Poverty? Yes. But not sadness.

It seemed they could always feel my stare. Our eyes would connect and a huge smile would envelop them. Seriously, their faces would completely light up. They had the most natural, peaceful smiles I had ever seen that reflected joy in their whole countenance. I was embarrassed. Here I was coming to their country to document their condition in order to produce empathy, and what I found was a strange feeling of jealousy… within me! I quickly recognized they had something I lacked—they had happiness.

It stung me. I faked a smile back pretending life was really as good for me as it appeared, but deep down I knew I was missing something.

I dismissed the feeling and concealed my shame. *I'm just as happy as they are,* I silently lied as I faked a smile to reassure myself. *Sure, I could be happier, but I haven't "found" it yet.*

I spent the next nine years searching for, working for, yearning for, and hungering for happiness. What a waste.

This book is written so you don't have to wait nine years. So you don't make the same mistakes I made. So you don't waste time and energy and money searching for, working for, and waiting for something that can't be found, bought, earned, or won.

Happiness, I have come to learn (thanks to the scientific research of top-tier universities) is more than a mood or a feeling—it's a skill.

Have you yearned for happiness? Or *more* happiness? Have you told yourself those misguided lies of, "I'll be happy when… I get a new car… or a bigger house… or a lover… or a better… whatever"? Have you felt there's more life out there for you? More passion, satisfaction, peace, and enjoyment? Have you looked at your house or apartment full of stuff and yet felt deep inside that there is something missing? That there's a hollowness or emptiness within you that needs to be filled?

If so then you will find great value in this book. Imagine what life would be like if your relationships were long lasting and more fulfilling. What if every Sunday night you didn't look at the clock with a sigh and dread the coming workweek ahead. Think what it would be like to feel loved and valued and needed. Picture yourself jumping out of bed in the morning excited for what the day might bring and then retiring each night pleased with what you were able to contribute. Imagine if adversity didn't throw you into a tailspin, if you were not easily distraught by life's challenges, and if you had more peace and contentment in your life.

Sounds like a bit of a stretch? That's what I thought until I have both interviewed uncommonly happy people who enjoy this kind of lifestyle and have embraced it myself.

They say you don't know what you don't know until you know. Maybe you're like me. I never would have said I was unhappy. I didn't think I was. *Moody maybe, but not unhappy*. It wasn't until I experienced the change that comes from learning to take deliberate, conscious control of my mental focus and choose my mindset that the world began to open up for me. Now I understand the difference. I look back at that decade of darkness in my life and with clarity see how easily they could have been the ten best years. The years are not regrets, though. They have allowed me to create a system that, when people follow it, almost always helps them enjoy a life filled with purpose and meaning.

What's especially helpful is that this is all based on science. Top-tier universities like Harvard, Stanford, The University of Pennsylvania and U.C. Berkley have been studying remarkably happy people to see what makes them tick. What qualities do they possess that make them exceptional? Why is it they are more resilient to life's challenges? But most importantly, they've been studying how regular people like you and I can replicate their results.

What they've found is that happiness is a skill. That means it's something that can be taught, tracked, stretched, incentivized, and improved.

Seven Core Skills of Happiness have emerged. Skills that, when applied consistently and regularly, almost always produce lasting happiness. These are the skills you can master to bring about everyday happiness.

You get that concept right? Not the kind of happiness that you have to wait for. That only comes on the weekends. After a major purchase. Once in a great while. Or when you're doing something exhilarating… Everyday happiness. The kind of peace, joy, and contentment you can enjoy each and every day, wherever you are, and in whatever circumstances you find yourself. It's the kind of happiness that springs from becoming more alive and awake. The happiness that comes from being more in control of your life.

This book is dedicated to the many "poor" people of Cambodia who showed me in their joyful faces that they were far wealthier than I in terms of what truly matters. And the book is also dedicated to those actively seeking a life of greater purpose, meaning, and satisfaction… those who are joining me on this amazing journey.

May you begin to truly flourish as we start this journey together. A journey that will bring out the best in you and the most in your life.

FOREWORD BY DR. LAPLANTE

IT'S A PRIVILEGE FOR ME TO INTRODUCE THIS revolutionary book. Revolutionary because of the concepts illustrated mixed with the methodology contained therein. You may observe that many books on the study of human potential leave you with a passion to implement good notions learned, but few provide concrete, achievable strategies to put them into long-term practice. *The 7 Core Skills of Everyday Happiness* describes in detail the 7 research-based pillars of happiness, but also transforms them into practical, step-by-step challenges to help you make small, incremental adjustments to attain a happier life. In addition, the author has created a portable smartphone application that parallels his book and helps you implement and measure changes in your overall happiness levels. This book is a therapeutic and transforming opportunity to help you regain control of your thought patterns and channel them in more productive directions. Not only will you experience a positive change, but those around will also experience the second-hand impact of your increased happiness.

Recent attention on positive psychology research has demonstrated a multitude of physical and psychological benefits associated with happiness. From boosted energy levels to increased longevity, studies on positive psychology denote the remarkable benefits of a happier life. One of my areas of expertise is the management of chronic pain. According to Melzak's Neuromatrix Theory of Pain (1999), negative emotions accentuate pain whereas positive emotions can mitigate the experience of pain. Studies have found techniques such as using humor and laughter to release endorphins (i.e., natural painkillers) can counter negative emotions, thus leading to the relief of pain. Watching a simple comedy clip prior to surgery has shown to help subjects be more relaxed, require less pain medication, and shorten the time required for the surgical procedure. The old adage "Laughter is the best medicine" might be true for pain management, but emerging literature on happiness expands the benefits of a positive mindset to many facets of life.

In my career as a clinical psychologist, I have had the opportunity to work with complex conditions. One of those is posttraumatic stress disorder—also known as PTSD. I worked with a particular worker who was involved in an explosion that severely burned his face as well as injured his back. He was incredibly traumatized. His hands, arms, and legs would shake uncontrollably; he would start sweating when he discussed any aspect of his traumatic accident. The memory of the experience controlled his life and caused him to avoid many situations, people, and activities that reminded him of the explosion. Each night he would wake up screaming in horror due to terrible nightmares. He reported that his altered physical appearance was the least of his problems when compared to his emotional turmoil. He had lost hope for a normal life.

To his surprise, the treatment was successful and resulted in ending his nightmares about his accident, his avoidance of triggers, his extreme physiological arousal, and his rapid influx of irritability. He could watch movies involving explosions; he could drive by the site of the accident; he could talk to his old boss; he was again capable of nurturing his relationship with his fiancée.

You may think the treatment was very complex. Actually, it was not. While some of the treatment involved education about PTSD and establishing trust, the most effective part of his treatment focused on empowering him with simple anxiety management techniques as well as strategies to challenge beliefs and thoughts about his trauma. Small challenges were designed to allow his brain to reprocess the trauma while permitting him to regain the confidence needed to overcome his fears. As one of his fears was associated with fire, a hierarchy of challenges was created around exposure to flames. It started by looking at campfire pictures and gradually built up to the final test: visiting the site where the explosion occurred. Accomplishing these simple steps permitted the adequate reprocessing of information and helped him intentionally modify his thought patterns, which led him to increased physical and mental health.

Taking constant small, often seemingly insignificant steps in a positive direction has the potential to produce colossal changes. This is what I've noted in the hundreds of clients I've successfully treated during the course of therapy. The methodology I've followed closely parallels the underlying methodology in *The 7 Core Skills of Everyday Happiness.*

Just like my burn patient whose thought processes limited his ability to function adequately, many people unknowingly find themselves spiraling downward due to a myriad of distorted thoughts and perceptions they feel are outside of their control. They feel confined in their circumstances, which frequently result in stress responses, anxiety, and depression. Often, the solution is simpler than expected. Identifying distorted thoughts and systematically rectifying them through small, conscious mental efforts will reform the thought process and engender new pathways. This therapeutic approach is called cognitive therapy.

While the book is founded on the innovative principles of positive psychology, I believe the 7 core skills of everyday happiness could also be referred to as positive cognitive therapy. In the past, the focus of psychology was predominantly aimed at reducing psychological symptomatology. Dr. Kerry Mothersill (2016), former president of the Canadian Psychological Association, published an article citing the need to enhance positivity in cognitive-behavioral therapy. Mothersill emphasized this shift was necessary due to the emerging research supporting the role of positive emotional regulation on health outcomes, the effectiveness of positive emotions and cognitions on psychopathology, the neurological processing of negative and positive emotions, and the effectiveness of positive psychology interventions. Wilhite has bridged this gap by facilitating the deliberate focus on and creation of positive cognitions. Traditional cognitive therapy promotes the alteration of faulty, negative thought patterns, but this book will encourage you to mold your cognitive processes to create a positive mindset. Just as continually challenging negative thoughts can defeat depression; mindfully forging positive thoughts will create patterns for lasting happiness.

Repetition is key in altering cognitive processes. Frequent reminders, a desire to achieve change, and small attempts to improve your abilities are all that is required to start building your happiness skills. Newborn children will gradually develop the physical abilities necessary to walk; PTSD patients will be required to actively participate in completing a hierarchy of therapeutic assignments; and individuals seeking to optimize their happiness also need to develop happiness skillsets. Practice does make perfect. A deliberate, constant, and regular implementation of the innovative concepts presented in *The 7 Core Skills of Everyday Happiness* will alter your life, and positively impact the lives of those around you.

— Dr. Christian Laplante, Ph.D., R. Psych, M.F.T.

Melzack, R. (1999). From the gate to the neuromatrix. *Pain*, 6, 121-126.

Mothersill, Kerry (2016), Enhancing positivity in cognitive behavioural therapy. *Canadian Psychology/Psychologie canadienne*, 57(1), 1-7.

"It isn't what you have or who you are or where you are or what you are doing that makes you happy or unhappy. It is what you think about it."
— *Dale Carnegie*

CHAPTER 1

HAPPINESS IS A SKILL

IT TOOK MERE SECONDS FOR ME TO GIVE UP HOPE. We were caught in the churn of the waves and the unrelenting pull of the rip current. I've never felt so powerless so quickly. *Three of us are going to die*, I determined. *This will surely put a damper on the family vacation.*

We had come to Lincoln City with my wife's sister's family. The kids were similar in ages and enjoyed playing together. The ocean always has a magical pull for children, beckoning them to play. This was especially true for my children who grew up in the Rocky Mountains far away from the sea.

It was the 5th of July. While technically summer, somehow it did not feel that warm on the Oregon coast. I had no desire to get wet, but I had a foreboding feeling about the kids playing in the ocean so I stayed nearby, watching cautiously.

The children were enjoying playing a game of "catch me if you can" with the ocean waves. You've probably played this yourself where you step out in ankle-deep water as far as you can then see how fast you can run back in before the larger waves come to get you wet. Each time you go back out, you're tempted by the seductive lure of the ocean to go deeper and further taunt the sea with your speed. As you know, inevitably the ocean always wins.

Having gotten distracted, I looked up to see my oldest daughter and her counterpart cousin screaming as they were being pulled out into the breaking waves. I called for help and quickly threw my jacket on the ground with my wallet and phone. In an instant I was in the water. It didn't take me long to reach Jordan. Getting her back in to shore would prove much more difficult. The undertow of the current and the churn of the waves were unbelievably powerful. My strength was quickly spent, but somehow I got Jordan back close enough to shore that she could walk again. I turned back out and saw that her mother had also jumped in to save her but was now caught in the same predicament being tossed around furiously like a ragdoll. My own daughter was even further out to sea.

Ignoring any sort of scout training, I jumped back in to do what I could. By the time I got to my sister-in-law, our strength was wiped out. The crashing waves threw us around so violently it was difficult to tell which way was even up. I was certain the three of us would die. Hope was gone.

That's when the most unexpected thing happened. I saw my daughter standing up in the water. She was south of us in waist-deep water waving to us to come towards her. Another wave crashed on top of us and turned us around but we could still see her standing and beckoning. We focused on her and put all our remaining energy into swimming towards my daughter. Surprisingly, the pull of the undertow suddenly lessened and our feet struck a sandbar. We were saved.

It turns out we were caught in a rip current. According to the National Ocean Service, rip currents are narrow channels of fast-moving water that can move faster than an Olympic swimmer. They point out that panicked swimmers often try fighting a rip current by swimming straight back to the shore, which puts them at risk of drowning because of fatigue. NOAA counsels that they should instead swim parallel to the shore to get out of the current.

My daughter had struggled until her strength was spent then she turned as a last resort to the only stroke she knew well—the backstroke. By doing this she had gotten herself turned around and swam south to safety.

Why do I share this story? Because sometimes we need to go in a completely unexpected direction to get where we want to go. We all want to be happy. In fact, if you look at the heart of each one of your choices, you'll see that you made them because you thought it would make you happier. Most everything we do in life we do with the belief it will make us happy.

Generally, we're wrong.

Things we think will make us happy strangely don't. The more we struggle and fight the more exhausted and discouraged we can become.

Within the pages of this book you will be presented with ideas and concepts that at first glance may seem like the wrong direction or the wrong intensity. Keep an open mind. Sometimes it's the simple things (like calmly floating along with the backstroke) that unexpectedly get us out of trouble and back to safety.

Like the boiling waves, life can be filled with turmoil. There may come times of adversity, doubt, discouragement or misfortune. Don't lose hope. An ocean of research from top-tier universities has revealed the most amazing and surprising thing about happiness—

They've found happiness is a skill.

THE OPTIMIST'S UNFAIR ADVANTAGE

You've met people who have an unfair advantage. The rich naturally get richer. Smart kids get into honors classes and are given scholarships and opportunities unavailable to the "regular" class of students. Get enough gifted athletic people on the same team and success for them is obvious and expected. The same holds true for optimists. But their advantage extends into all aspects of life—money, relationships, self-confidence, social fulfillment, and overall life satisfaction.

Think of the most optimistic person you know. Picture them in your head so clearly that you can see their face and hear their laugh. Have you ever wondered how they got like that? Are they successful because they're so optimistic or is it the other way around? Have you noticed how everything seems to go right for them? That's how it seems anyway because even when things go wrong, somehow it doesn't faze them. They don't appear stressed or worried. They laugh a lot. They seem to have the best relationships. Friends flock to them. They're a joy to be around. And even though we're envious of their lifestyle, still we love being around optimistic people like that.

If you're anything like I was, living a life like that was a distant wish. A dream.

Well, I've got good news for you. Optimism can be trained. Success is a mindset. And while life can sometimes be so unfair, fortunately it can be unfair in your favor.

You are on your way to enjoying a happier, more energetic, more positive life, the kind you've always wished you could have.

You are going to love this book. You're going to love how it makes you feel. You're going to love how it opens your mind to possibilities. You're going to love how simple and easy it is to make profound change in your life. The good kind. The kind that will, in positive ways, impact every area of your life—your hopes, your happiness, your relationships, your drive, the way you handle stress and anxiety—seriously, this is going to be life-changing.

And what's so life-changing about this is that it's going to help you take active, deliberate control of your thoughts. Since thoughts precede everything else, it makes sense that this has the power to create positive impact in all aspects of your life.

LIGHTLY LEASHED ELEPHANTS

Let me illustrate. You've heard the phrase, "An elephant never forgets," right? They've studied elephants and found they have amazing memories. For example, they can remember other elephants they knew briefly twenty years ago. But what's truly amazing is how their memories can be used … against them.

Let me tell you a story.

Brian Tracy tells this. He said[1], "When elephant trainers in India catch a baby elephant, they tie one of its legs to a post with a rope. The baby elephant struggles and struggles but can't get free. For days the elephant pulls and strains at the rope. Gradually, it learns that struggle is useless and it gives up.

"When the elephant grows up, the trainer keeps it tied to the same rope in the same way. And even though it can now break the rope and get away, it stands passively and waits for the trainer to come and get it."

Imagine that. Picture one of these enormously powerful animals out in the jungle. It has the capacity to uproot trees with its trunk, but it can be lightly leashed because it's been trained into a state of "learned helplessness". Through negative experiences, it has learned that struggling is useless and it gives up trying.

Martin Seligman, the father of positive psychology, pointed out this state of "learned helplessness" can be found in people as we've been repeatedly conditioned through negative experiences. We get into a state of mind where our growth stagnates because we don't believe change is possible.

It's not your fault if you feel that way. You've done nothing wrong. You've been *conditioned* into this state of learned helplessness. However, we are going to fix that. You're like that elephant that never forgets. You are powerful. You are capable. Together, we will remove these self-imposed limitations by helping you remember the capacity you have within.

The awesome thing about this book on the 7 Core Skills of Everyday Happiness is that it's all based on the scientific research of positive psychology led by top-tier universities. This revolutionary new branch within psychology has exploded in the past twenty years. Now Harvard, the University of Pennsylvania, Columbia, Stanford, and U.C. Berkley all offer masters degrees in this exciting new arm of psychology, a branch that focuses on the science of human flourishing.

I want to point out that the book is really about mindset conditioning. Mental training at its best. Each chapter, each section, is designed to help you deliberately, consciously choose what you focus on. We're going to help you concentrate on concentrating. Think about how you're thinking. You're going to learn to choose your thoughts rather than have them chosen for you because of circumstances or conditioning, habit or outward appearances. You're going to gain the power to control your thoughts. With this clarity and as you come to master your mindset, the world will open up to you.

Now, how does this relate to happiness? Happiness is the main benefit. It's the main motivating factor in our lives. Think about it. Whenever you make a choice generally you do so because you hope it will make you happy. Why did you choose those clothes you're wearing? *Because I thought they'd make me more attractive.* Why did you want that? *So I would get the approval of others.* Why did you want approval? *So I would be included... Ok... I get it... So I would be happy.*

Happiness really is at the heart of everything we strive for. So with this mindset conditioning we've turned things around. We're going to help you reprogram your mindset by focusing on the things that will bring happiness. Then all the other good things you want in life will fall into place.

Can you see why I'm so excited for you? Can you see how life-changing this is going to be? Each day that you spend learning the materials and applying them will pay off with huge dividends.

You are in the driver seat.

Go at your own pace, but remember the application of the principles is key. If you participate in one of my online courses, you will find they come with daily activities. Do 'em. They will help you make small, incremental adjustments to your thinking. Repetition is key. You don't achieve a healthy physical life by doing two push-ups or after a single day at the gym. A healthy mental lifestyle is similarly achieved by deliberate, conscious activity repeatedly done. I suggest you use the reminder system in the Feed Your Happy app or a reminder feature that may be in your phone to remind you every day at a set time to login and participate.

That's where the name for the Feed Your Happy app came from. We're nourished properly with daily feeding. It's the same thing with our mindset conditioning. The more consistently and regularly you repeat your mindset conditioning the more your reactions will become natural and instinctive, but, most importantly, positive.

You can do it. Step by step. Little by little. Optimism can be trained. Happiness is a skill. And the secret to truly flourishing is to control your mindset so you can avoid harmful thinking and, instead, deliberately choose to focus on thoughts that will produce a happier, more successful, more fulfilling life.

Let life be unfair in your favor.

"Change your thoughts and you change your world."
— *Norman Vincent Peale*

CHAPTER 2

THE ROAD TO A MORE FULFILLING LIFE

YOU'RE DOING THE BEST THINK YOU CAN POSSIBLY DO for yourself—you're taking time to deliberately focus, to intentionally concentrate; you are learning to control and master what you think about. Consider how each day we have so many thoughts that pass through our heads. We're conditioned to respond and to react. Our work environments, our home and social lives can feel chaotic, which can rub off on our mental and emotional states. How often do we stop and separate ourselves from the chaos in order to deliberately, intentionally take back control over our mental state?

Right? Yeah, you're in the right place. And this book is so going to help you out.

TINY BITS OF RUST

Before I get into introducing myself, let me tell you a story. This happened when I was first married. I had this little Honda car. It was the perfect car for newlyweds, a little four-door Accord. Well, one day it started developing this problem where it would sputter and jerk around whenever you'd put on the brake. Really, it was whenever we let off the gas and let it idle. It would chug and chug and chug … and sometimes die. We had to continually keep the car revved up. You can imagine how tricky this sputtering would be when we got to an intersection to turn left.

Since we shared the car, I worried about the safety of my new bride. I took the car to the dealership; they found little tiny bits clogging the carburetor. $250 bucks. Yikes. That was a lot for a young college student. But the worst part is the problem returned two weeks later. I took it back to the dealership; they wanted another $250 to clean the carburetor again … because they found bits in there again. I was furious to find they were content to keep treating symptoms but didn't bother to look deeper to find out what the real problem was—the cause. It turns out the gas tank had rusted inside and was sending rust into the system, clogging the carburetor.

That's what we're doing here in this book. We're jumping to the heart of what's causing or, more correctly, amplifying the problems in your life … what's getting things clogged in *your* system. But not only that, we're addressing what's limiting you from achieving even greater success. It all starts in your mind with the mindset you choose or allow yourself to have.

Thomas A. Edison said, "If we did all the things we are capable of, we would literally astound ourselves." It all starts with our thoughts.

Hi. I'm Scott Wilhite. I'm an award-winning commercial filmmaker, a writer, producer, and director. I'm the founder of nCOURAGE.LIFE. I'm a social entrepreneur. And I'm the creator of the Feed Your Happy™ app.

When I learned about the transformational power that comes by deliberately, intentionally choosing what I focus on mentally, it was amazing. Seriously life-changing. Although I had been extremely "successful" creatively, it was empty. I felt this void in my life. This hollowness that consumed me. And it was crazy too because I had almost everything I desired. I had a beautiful, wonderful wife, four awesome kids who didn't fight, we lived in a quiet neighborhood up in the mountains, and I had a job creating commercials and films, which is exactly what I love to do. Still, there was this strange feeling that said I wasn't living up to my potential. That I had more to give but no outlet to actually do that. I felt stuck and trapped. I felt unsatisfied … and I'm embarrassed to admit … I felt unhappy.

Now, I didn't know I was unhappy at the time. I mean I knew I was not satisfied but I thought that was just part of my personality. I thought I was a "tortured artist" and that that was just the way I was programmed. I accepted the mindset of *That's the baggage you get from being in the creative field.*

So when I learned about the emerging science that's come from the field of positive psychology, I can't express how my life began to change. It's like I came awake. I came alive.

It was like the feeling I had when I first fell in love with the woman who would become my wife, and I suddenly noticed how the world was more vibrant. There were more colors and more beauty that I hadn't noticed before. I suddenly became aware of this and enjoyed this euphoria for a week or two when I first fell in love. Maybe you've experienced this too. (I do want to note here that we naturally adapt to new conditions—unfamiliar locations soon become commonplace, devastating losses become bearable, and loving relationships may wane over time—but this book will also show you how to keep that excitement, spark, and zest for life and love alive by deliberately applying behavioral activation practices.)

So when I learned and started applying the principles of positive psychology, not only did I experience this re-awakening again but I also found that it was completely under my control.

No longer was the beauty of life, joy and happiness and this amazing feeling of coming alive dependent on my environment or my circumstances. No longer was it something I had to wait for. Or hope for. Or win. Or earn. Or buy. Happiness and the joy of life was now completely within my control as long as I chose my mindset. As long as I allowed myself to be in control.

And the cool thing was that now I knew I could spark my own happiness whenever and wherever I wanted.

When I learned this and saw the enormous difference this brought in my life, my next thought was that I wanted to share this with others. To have them feel what I feel and gain the control over their lives the way I had experienced. That was the genesis for what I'm doing now. What we're doing here together.

I hope you enjoy this book. That you experience an awakening. That you find more control over your life and the circumstances around you. I hope your relationships become more satisfying. That you find more zest in your life. Most importantly, I hope you discover purpose and meaning in your life and that you have the courage to then live it fully.

Imagine what life will be like for you then.

Optimism can be trained. Optimism is a state of mind. Sure, some lucky people come by it naturally, but the science has come to show it's available to all of us—if we want it enough to actually DO something. To be active. In control. And deliberate.

This book and the related course are all about mindset training. Mental conditioning at its best. The Seven Core Skills of Everyday Happiness are based on the scientific research of top-tier universities who have been studying uncommonly happy people. Harvard, Penn State, Columbia, and U. Cal. Berkley are all pioneers in this amazing new branch of psychology. They've discovered that happiness is more than just a mood or a feeling—it's a skill.

As we strive to upskill your happiness, you will find you can achieve greater levels of success in ALL aspects of your life. People who truly thrive, who, as the scientists say, "flourish," find success universally.

Could true success be anything less? Imagine having the kind of relationships that are deep and satisfying. Imagine starting or ending each day grateful for what you have instead of being consumed by something you feel you lack. Can you see yourself ridding yourself of stress, and anxiety, and worry? Can you see the self-confidence you'll have as you make improvements daily? Imagine what you could do if you conquered fear and doubt.

Yes, this is mindset training. Yes, this is completely focused on you achieving greater success. And, yes, happiness—EVERYDAY happiness—is the main benefit that will come if you actively apply the skills and science presented in this book and online course.

I'm so glad you've invested in yourself.

BEST PRACTICES

Now, before we go too much further I want to point out some important concepts and techniques we employ that are designed to help you be more successful at not only learning these valuable mindsets but also, more importantly, putting them into daily practice. We've structured this for you to achieve astounding success.

First off, I want to explain timing. We've divided all the training up into bite-sized chunks. While it may be tempting to blast through this whole book to "learn" everything we have to share on mindset conditioning, the important thing is to actually *apply* the concepts. Knowing is different from doing. You will find much greater value if you take the time to soak in each lesson and then put the concept into practice. We're talking about mental conditioning and training, not reading and comprehension.

I remember when I first learned about all the research on positive psychology. Each night I would read every book I could find on the subject. It was temporarily transformative. I found I could change my focus from being consumed with everything I felt I was missing in life to actually enjoying what I had already been blessed with. I was able to rid myself of stress, anxiety, and worry by rewriting the hypothetical stories I was telling myself that always seemed to have such terrible endings. And I was able to find peace and serenity by learning to be in and stay in the moment. It was transformative—temporarily.

Then I found myself drifting back into my old ways of thinking. Nightly reading was great but I needed something that would help me out in the heat of the day when I was faced with the challenges of daily life. I realized I needed to train my brain to not only learn the concepts but to put them into practice regularly in order to turn them into a lifestyle. That's where the genesis of the Feed Your Happy app came from and the online conditioning courses we offer that systemize mindset training.

Regular, consistent, repeated mental exercises are key. You're training your brain to focus. The best way to consume this book is a small section at a time. Read a concept. Think about it. Apply it. Then repeat it until the idea and the actions become second nature for you. If you can't resist the temptation to blast through the book, do so with an understanding that you're doing so to get an overview then start back at the beginning and take each concept a day at a time, allowing yourself to properly focus on a single idea until it totally soaks in.

Where mental conditioning differs from physical weight training or aerobic conditioning is in the fact that it doesn't take much time to get an effective workout. Ten minutes a day will do wonders.

Now, where physical and mental conditioning are completely similar is in the fact that repetition reaps the greatest benefits. A couple of sit-ups or pushups or a single day at the gym will not do much for improving your physical fitness; however, a consistent, regular workout routine will bring great success. It's the repetition and consistency that's going to make the difference for you.

Please decide how much and how often you want to work out then set a reminder; I suggest you do it right now.

You can use the Feed Your Happy app to set reminders for yourself on which days and what times you'd like to be reminded to "Feed Your Happy" ('cause that's what we're doing here). Or, if you don't have the app, you can set a reminder in your smartphone to go off at a consistent time each day. Do this now. I can't stress that enough.

You decide when and how often you read a new section of this book—when you want to do your mental workouts. I will caution you, though, that if you don't decide right now and make a plan, your development may get sidetracked on the road of good intentions. This isn't news for you. Think about when you've had plans to get into shape physically or made some New Year's resolution but went back to your normal routine because you hadn't made a concrete plan, set a specific time, or properly developed a consistent routine. Let's make this successful for you.

Right now, set a recurring reminder using your smartphone or the Feed Your Happy app.

One more note on repetition. First, of course, there's the consistency in the regularity with which you learn the lessons, we just talked about that. The second part of repetition is in the concepts themselves. You will find we deliberately repeat ideas and themes throughout this book in order to further engrain them into your mind. You've been conditioned for years by society or by circumstance to think and react a certain way. It will take time, consistency, and repetition to reverse or rewrite the conditioning you've endured.

Many activities are suggested in this book. The online course offers more and provides a systemized approach for regular, repeated participation. Do not skip them or do them half-heartedly. And when you're prompted to journal responses, do not take the easy road and write the same reactions multiple days in a row. Don't take the path of least resistance. Grow. Stretch. Allow yourself time to think and contemplate. Use repetition with the activities to stretch, to dig deeper, to think harder and to come up with new responses. The more effort you put in the more results you'll get out.

FIGHTER PILOT TRAINING

I have a friend who is an Air Force fighter pilot. He flies F-16s. When he was in training he showed me his flight suit, which had a flat section right above the knee for his flight book or flight manual.

He told me that they would practice drills over and over and over again on what to do in case of different emergencies. The procedures were contained in the book, and he would wear the book so he could regularly and repeatedly go through the exercises while in the cockpit.

He said they practiced them so much and so often … so that if an actual emergency were to come, he would naturally and instinctively know what to do without ever consulting the book.

This matches up with what Navy ace, Lieutenant Bill "Willy" Driscoll pointed out once. He said, "In combat, a fighter pilot always expects to 'rise to the occasion', but in fact he will always fall back to his level of training." Creating positive routines will help you weather the unforeseen challenges ahead by conditioning your brain to instinctively avoid the ruts and seek the higher ground.

MENTAL TRIGGERS

I want to explain a mindset technique we will be training you to use. We're helping you train with mental triggers. These are concepts, stories, and ideas that have a strong visual image associated with them. When you see one of these mental triggers it will remind you of the story associated with them and you can then use that memory as the spark to deliberately control your mental focus.

For example, I know a guy who went from a scarcity mentality, where he was always feeling poor and believed that he would forever be poor, to a mindset of faith where he believed God was providing for him and that God had an abundance of resources with which to provide. One of the mental triggers he set for himself was that when he saw a coin on the ground he would think to himself, *God is my provider, and He's got such an abundance it's even spilling out into the street.*

Pretty cool, right? He used a simple, visual trigger to then spark a mindset he would like to be in. The mindset he'd chosen. By repeatedly putting himself in this mindset, he has been able to build his faith and trust, and have control over choosing to have a mindset of abundance. (And, yes, it's had a profound impact on his financial status as well as his daily feelings of peace and security).

Throughout the book, we will help you gain mental triggers of your own that you can then apply to deliberately concentrate on the mindsets you would like to internalize.

"People generally see what they look for, and hear what they listen for."
— Harper Lee

CHAPTER 3

IT STARTS IN THE MINDSET

BEFORE WE GET INTO THE 7 CORE SKILLS OF EVERYDAY Happiness, it's best that we get an understanding of our current mindsets. Let's look at how we may have been conditioned to think and explore some of the misconceptions about happiness. With a proper assessment of where we're at, we are then better prepared to move forward.

THE THREE MINDSETS OF SUCCESS

Note: I elaborate on this more in my three-part video series, The 3 Mindsets of Success. As a book owner, you can find free access to this course on my website: www.nCOURAGE.LIFE/3mindsets

The first mindset of success is the Limited Mindset. It's the mindset that actually limits our success. Sure, we can achieve some amounts of success with this, but not as much as we could if we didn't put limits on ourselves. Limiting mindsets are where we let our doubts or fears take over. We tell ourselves these limiting stories like, "I'm not good with numbers, I'm a terrible salesman, I'm not athletic, I'll never get married, I'm just a mechanic, she always forgets about me, rich people always rip me off, I could never speak in public," or the ever-so-confining story, "I'm shy." These stories are fictional but can prove to be self-fulfilling prophecies the more we tell, retell, and believe them. This mindset confines you within an ever-shrinking playing field. But once you recognize that you're telling yourself limiting stories, you then have the opportunity to remove those limits.

This is done by rewriting the restricting stories we tell ourselves, which moves us into the second mindset of success—the Growth Mindset. This is the belief mindset where you believe there are greater possibilities out there for you than what appears on the surface. This is where you believe you are a work in progress; that you have great potential. You also believe that roadblocks are not dead ends; that circumstances don't determine your fate. You are full of possibilities and the world is open with opportunities.

This is not delusional. It's not tricking our brains or fooling ourselves. This growth mindset is a product of voluntarily and repeatedly focusing on positive expectations you desire then acting on that faith. The growth mindset is about allowing ourselves to believe that better things are coming.

With a growth mindset you say, "I am adventurous or brave. I am smart. I can learn new things. I'm imaginative. I'm enthusiastic. I am eternally curious." You can see how these don't have confined endings. It's like the difference between an open-ended or a closed-ended question. A closed question is, "How was your day?" Why even ask that question, right? The answer is always, "Fine," even if the day was horrible. An open-ended question is, "Will you tell me about your day?" Now the other person can go on for hours telling all about their day.

I want you to have an open-ended life. I want you to enjoy a growth mindset and believe in the possibilities of you. Don't tell yourself confining, limiting stories about yourself like, "I'm only a mechanic," or, "I can't remember names," "I could never be a public speaker," or, "I'm fat."

I hesitate tackling this self-defeating story because it sounds so, so, so negative, but it's one that I believe far too many of us tell ourselves and I'd like to eradicate it.

Even if you do have a few more pounds on you that you'd like to get rid of, don't tell yourself a limiting story like that. You can see how that statement has a concluding ending, Right? Because you're saying, "Right now. Today. And forever I'm fat." And generally when people tell this to themselves they stretch out that word like air was somehow leaking out of them—"I'm phaaaaaaat." Instead, deliberately choose a growth mindset. This can be done with a simple change of words... Even if you don't remove that super-negative, incredibly limiting word (which I would suggest you would), you can say, "Currently I'm fat," and you can COMPLETELY change your story.

I would suggest something more inspiring like, "Currently I've got a few more pounds than I care for." The important thing is to change the story from a closed story to an open story. I hope you can see how adding in the word "Currently" suddenly opens up your story to, "OK, right now this is my condition ... but it's obviously not my FINAL condition." *Currently* is NEVER the end of any story.

Learn to put yourself in a growth mindset and you will achieve much more success.

By removing your limiting mindset and fueling your personal beliefs to have faith in possibilities, you set the stage for the third and most effective mindset of success—the Deliberate Mindset. This is the mindset where you take active control of your life... Of your thoughts and belief systems. The deliberate mindset is the heart of everything you will learn in this book or do in The 7 Core Skills of Everyday Happiness course. It's about deliberately, intentionally choosing what you focus on. It's about putting things into motion. Not being a spectator in your life, but taking the role of being an active participant.

More than anything else, choosing to put yourself in a deliberate mindset will get you on the road to Everyday Happiness.

THE SCIENCE OF HAPPINESS

If you've got the mindset that happiness is just a nice, warm feeling, you'll be surprised to know it's much, much more. In recent years there's been a staggering amount of research done that shows happiness improves employee performance on nearly every level. According to world-renowned positive psychology researcher Sonja Lybomirsky, happier people are:[2]
- More productive
- More creative
- Better team leaders
- They make better negotiators

- They take less sick days
- They are more resilient
- They recover faster from injuries
- They make more money
- They are more likely to get a raise

I'm starting with the financial benefits of happiness because we've been conditioned by society that that's what "success" is. We'll give a nod to this old way of thinking as we slowly embrace true human flourishing.

You may be interested in the health benefits of happiness.

The US Surgeon General has been going around prescribing happiness. Isn't that awesome? As the chief medical officer for the United States, Dr. Vivek Murthy travels around the country not promoting proper diet and exercise but pleading with people to improve their happiness levels[3]. He says, "Happiness affects us on a biological level. It lowers stress hormones as well as inflammatory markers. Even when you control for smoking, physical activity and other health behaviors, it turns out happier people live longer." He also points out that there's something we can do about our happiness.

Here are the scientifically proven benefits of happiness[4]
- Feel better
- Boosts your energy
- Boosts your creativity
- Improves your immune system
- Bolsters your cardiovascular system
- Enjoy better relationships
- Have higher productivity
- Live longer
- More social
- More charitable
- More cooperative
- More hopeful
- Better liked by others
- Less materialistic
- Higher self-confidence
- Higher self-esteem
- Considered more attractive

Not a bad list of benefits, right? Can you see why when we do this mindset conditioning we focus on training your mind to allow yourself to be happy? You win all around.

Let's take a deeper dive now into some of the science; some of the research done lately that substantiates some of these benefits. Let me tell you about "The Nun Study".[5]

THE NUN STUDY

This study was led by researcher David A. Snowden. They studied six hundred and seventy-eight nuns in seven convents. These are women who had the most similar lifestyle you can imagine. They were standardized. They ate the same food, had the same occupations, did the same exercise routines, had the same sleep patterns, and lived in the same place.

What was different was their attitude.

When the women were in their twenties they were asked to write their autobiographies when they took their final vows. The autobiographies were later coded for positive and negative words. Those who expressed more positive emotions in their autobiographies lived significantly longer—generally ten years longer—than those expressing fewer positive emotions.

Get this. By age 80, sixty percent of the least positive nuns had died, compared to only twenty-five percent of the most positive.... Fifty-four percent of the happy nuns reached age 94, while only fifteen percent of the least happy nuns reached that age.

This is only one of a host of studies that show the longevity benefits of happiness. There are many other studies showing that being happy not only increases the quantity of our days but, more importantly, the quality. Think how much better your life will be since both your cardiovascular and immune systems can be improved through joyful living.

One more thing before we leave this lesson. Now, not only have you heard about the scientifically proven health, financial, and longevity benefits of happiness, but you're also getting clued into the fact that there's something you can do to elevate your own happiness levels. Happiness is a mindset. It's a choice.

Like the nuns in the study, we can have the same experiences, live in the same neighborhoods, and enjoy the same levels of wealth, but it is our attitude that will make the difference. Knowledge can be power if you apply that knowledge and turn it into wisdom.

"Happiness is not a state to arrive at, but a manner of traveling."
— *Margaret Lee Runbeck*

CHAPTER 4

THE MYTHS OF HAPPINESS

BY NOW YOU MAY BE THINKING, OK. *I get it. Everything is better if I'm happy—I'm healthier. I can live longer. And I can be more successful at work and in my relationships. But I've been searching for, working for, and yearning for happiness all my life—I don't get it... Why am I not happy, or at least as happy as I could be?*

It turns out we've been searching for happiness in all the wrong places. I know this for myself through dark, personal experience. I was caught in the trap. For an entire decade I was so insanely dissatisfied with my life. I felt there was more for me. More happiness. More peace. More joy. Contentment. Love. Adventure. Passion. Excitement. Fulfillment. Really, more LIFE out there somewhere for me. I was convinced I would find it in the next gig. Or the next big award. Or a new car. Nicer house. Or whatever. Happiness was elusive. The harder I worked the more out of reach happiness became. I was tired, worn down, and empty.

I realized feeling this way was completely crazy because I had a wonderful wife, four amazing kids, a nice house in a safe neighborhood, a good job that let me express myself creatively... I had everything but happiness. I mean I had it ... sort of. But deep down I knew there was something more. Something better. And it was just out of reach. Can you relate?

Now, I want to remind you that this is not your fault. You've been conditioned this way. I mentioned this earlier when I talked about how an elephant never forgets. Remember? Of course you do. You are as strong and powerful as an elephant, but you've been conditioned by limiting beliefs and these self-defeating stories we tell ourselves over and over again. You've been conditioned. Trained. Weakened, really. While it's not your fault that you've been conditioned this way, now that you know this, now that you can see what control you truly have in your life, it will be your fault if you continue and don't do something about it.

I know that's harsh for me to say but you get that, right? If an elephant were to suddenly realize the incredible strength he possesses, and looked at the puny rope that was keeping him confined, he would not allow himself to be lightly leashed by someone else, unless that was their choice. You are as powerful as that elephant. You have the choice. In everything you do, you can choose your mindset.

So let's talk about some of the Myths of Happiness.

MYTH #1 – HAPPINESS IS FOUND IN THINGS

We all know money doesn't buy happiness, but we still hope, right? We know it in our heads but not our hearts.

In the movie *Fiddler on the Roof* the adorable Tevye is told, "Money is the world's curse." To which Tevye responds, "May the Lord smite me with it, and may I never recover."

Sure, money may not bring happiness, but we all want to give it a go. Maybe it'll work for us, right?

So a question for you… To get this happiness you seek, are you more likely going to get it by winning the lottery or being involved in a terrible, crippling accident?

Instinctively, we think we know the answer. It's obvious, right? But here's some fun science done by Phillip Brickman and Dan Coates.[6]

They interviewed 22 major lottery winners. Seven won $1 million, six won $400,000, two won $300k, four won $100k, and three won fifty-thousand dollars. No bad, right? You'd like to be in their shoes, you're thinking.

Then they interviewed people who had been crippled for life—eleven paraplegic and eighteen quadriplegic victims.

Plus, they had a control group.

Now the questions. They asked them to rate how pleasant they found each of these 7 everyday activities:
- Talking with a friend
- Watching TV
- Eating breakfast
- Hearing a funny joke
- Receiving a compliment
- Reading a magazine
- Buying clothes

The lottery winners rated each activity lower than the control group. The victims also rated each activity lower than the control group but higher than the lottery winners.

The accident victims were not as unhappy as expected. They reported lower general happiness than the lottery winners, but their happiness levels were quite well above the middle of the scale.

The point is we think we know what will make us happy. And we're terrible judges. Still, we keep trying. Let's go for the money again.

In another study, this one done in 2008 at the University of California, Santa Barbara[7], they measured people's happiness levels six months after winning a modest lottery prize in Holland equivalent to eight months' worth of income. The study found it had no effect on happiness.

This money thing isn't working.

The problem comes as we look outside ourselves with this false belief that something external will make us happy. When we believe money, food, travel, or a life of leisure will somehow make us happy, this fictional belief is not substantiated by science, nor is it upheld by easy observation. How many extremely wealthy people do you know who are not happy? Or how many times have you heard about an exceptionally famous person who seems to have everything and yet they end up taking their own lives ... or they drink themselves away ... or fall into the trap of drug addiction as they strive to escape "everyday life"? It's sad.

Happiness is not found in things. It's a myth. And it's one that almost all of us get caught up in.

The great stand-up comedian Louis CK was on the Conan O'Brian Show talking about how "Everything is amazing and nobody is happy." He teases about people who complain about their airplane flights. He says, "People will come back from flights and they'll tell you their story ... and it's like a horror story. They act like their flight is like a cattle car in the '40s in Germany. (Then, imitating these people, he says) *It was the worst day of my life... First of all we didn't board for 20 minutes... And then we get on the plane and they make us sit there... ON THE RUNWAY for 40 minutes...*'" He laughs at them as he vents about the flaws in their myopic thinking... "Then what happens next, did you FLY IN THE AIR ... IN A CHAIR?"

His poking fun hits us to the core as we realize we are guilty of complaining like this. We have all these amazing technologies and conveniences and lifestyles, and yet we are incredibly ungrateful and dissatisfied. Am I right? We have computers that fit in our pocket. We have medicines that cure diseases that would have killed us a century ago. We live in an age of miracles. An age of wonders... Louis CK is right, "Everything's amazing and nobody's happy."

And why are we not happy? Because we've been conditioned to look for happiness outside of ourselves. So it's our thinking really that needs to change, not the fact that we need more or better or cooler stuff.

We've got to get our mindsets decontaminated. We've got to get our thinking cleared up so, when it comes time to deliberately focus on what is going right in our lives, we can do that with perfect clarity.

MYTH #2 – "I'LL BE HAPPY WHEN..."

The main myth we're working to debunk here is the myth that happiness exists outside of ourselves and that something ... or someone ... or at some amazing future event the world around us will suddenly change and everything will align, and it will make us happy.

Happiness isn't something that can be bought or earned or found or won. Happiness starts with our mindsets.

Let's talk about the myth of, "I'll be happy when…"

Have you fallen into the trap of telling yourself, "I'll be happy when…"? Maybe you've said, "I'll be happy when I find a lover…" or, "I'll be happy when we get married…" or, "I'll be happy when we start having kids…" or, "I'll be happy when these kids are out of diapers…" or, "I'll be happy when these kids move out…"

You see the flaw? Our lives pass by without us ever *being* happy.

Think about it. Whenever you say to yourself, "I'll be happy when…" you're telling yourself you're not happy *now*. You've created a story for yourself that you're not satisfied right now and that you will continue to be unsatisfied and unhappy until something remarkable changes. This fictional story takes happiness outside of yourself and keeps it outside of your control. Happiness with this sort of mindset is always a carrot-stick away.

What are some stories you've been telling yourself? Right now are you caught up in the "I'll be happy when…" cycle? Maybe you are looking forward to a graduation or a job promotion or summer or some event. Now think back, are there times you can remember when you've said those same words, "I'll be happy when…" for some thing or event? Did it truly change your life or was it merely temporary? Let's not go for temporary; let's build a mindset that lasts.

OK, let's talk briefly about the emptiness of attainment. We love setting goals and having things to look forward to, but often we find they don't hold as much satisfaction as we had hoped. Think about your experience with this. Maybe you were so looking forward to some monumental accomplishment. Maybe it was a graduation, or a completed project, or a fulfilled wish. Think about how that day seemed to fly by and you were on to your next monumental accomplishment, complicated project or soon-to-be-fulfilled wish. The joy comes in the journey. Not in the attainment.

Don't delay your happiness. Don't procrastinate it away. Don't get caught in the never-ending cycle of "I'll be happy when…" It's a myth.

Now, before I leave this topic, I want to point out that there's nothing wrong with looking forward to something. Absolutely … have things to look forward to. Have things to *hope* for and to *be excited* about. Anticipation is an awesome skill that you can use to spark your happiness levels. We'll talk more in-depth about specific ways you can use anticipation to generate happiness in Core Happiness Skill #2.

The key is to use anticipation deliberately. Use it as a tool to spark your happiness, which is completely different from being controlled by your thoughts of future events or being controlled by anything external. Remember the elephant? Don't be lightly leashed; you're in control.

I AM

There's a super interesting documentary film made by legendary comedy director Tom Shadyac. He created outrageously unruly films like *Ace Ventura: Pet Detective, Liar, Liar,* and *Bruce Almighty.* His films grossed nearly two billion dollars at the box office. He was living high and living large. Then he had a terrible mountain bike accident that made him rethink his life. The film is called, *I Am.* In this surprisingly sensitive documentary he talks about his rise to fame and wealth. At one point he moves into this amazing mansion and he has a realization as the movers are leaving him alone in his house and he's standing at the top of this beautiful staircase looking at his incredible entryway—he realizes it didn't make him happy.

I recommend the movie to anyone. It's an interesting exploration into happiness and the cause of the world's ills. I love his comparison about cancer of the mind and our thoughts of greed and selfishness. Check it out.

So… "I'll be happy when…" is a myth. The belief that "Happiness is found in things" is a myth. The third myth I want to point out is that something will *make us* happy.

MYTH #3 – _____ WILL MAKE US HAPPY

It's the same concept as understanding that anger is a choice. When little kids fight they rationalize their behavior with, "Well, he *made me* angry" or "She *made me* mad," which, of course, then means they can hit them or take their toy. Wise parents will identify this marred way of thinking and correct the downward spiral it can cause in a life.

Nobody can *make you* anything. You are an agent of choice. A being of choice. In any situation you can choose how you react. With the same situation you can choose to be angry or you can choose to be humored. You can choose to be frustrated by a thorny project or you can choose take a step away and look at it in a new light or from a new angle. You choose how you react.

Anger is a choice and so is happiness.

Contrary to your previous beliefs, chocolate cake won't *make you* happy… A new car won't *make you* happy… A sudden change in your circumstances or your environment won't *make you* either.

Viktor Frankl, in his powerful book, *Man's Search for Meaning*, talks about his experiences in a Nazi concentration camp. He says, "When we are no longer able to change a situation, we are challenged to change ourselves." Frankl witnessed in the horrors of those camps that there were people who had the courage to suffer and bear the most appalling, inhumane treatment, yet live lives true to themselves. Of these he said, "Everything can be taken from a man but one thing: the last of the human freedoms—to choose one's attitude in any given set of circumstances, to choose one's own way."

Something can happen that will trigger you to react with either anger or happiness, but ultimately you have the opportunity to choose or control how you will react.

You can learn to be present. You can train yourself to be authentically grateful. You can develop skills of generosity, compassion, and kindness. It's completely within your control. Can you see how happiness is in your hands right now? Imagine how much better your relationships will be as you learn to intentionally care for and serve others. Picture how many more friends will be attracted to you when you develop a positive outlook on life. Imagine how much better each day will be as you expect good things in your life instead of delaying your happiness with an "I'll be happy when…" mindset.

MYTH #4 – YOU'RE EITHER BORN WITH IT OR YOU'RE NOT

Optimism can be trained. It's also a myth that you're either born an optimist or you're not. And if you weren't born an optimist, well, you're out of luck. Rubbish. I'm living proof of that. As a commercial film producer, I've been trained to look for and expect the worst. When putting a shoot together I would obsess over my mental "What if" game. "What if the camera goes down ... or an actor doesn't show ... or a location falls through ... or the weather turns bad ... or whatever." I've been a fully-trained pessimist. Now that I've learned happiness is a skill, it has completely changed my life. I hope it changes or amplifies yours.

Now that we've cleared up a few of the misconceptions and myths of happiness, let's start building. Let's talk about awesome new discoveries within the scientific field of positive psychology.

CHAPTER 5

POSITIVE PSYCHOLOGY

THIS BOOK ON THE SEVEN CORE SKILLS OF EVERYDAY Happiness is based on the scientific research of positive psychology. Many top-tier universities are leading the charge with breakthrough research, such as Harvard, Columbia, Stanford, the University of Pennsylvania, and U. Cal Berkley.

So what is it? According to the Positive Psychology Institute in Sydney Australia, "Positive psychology is the scientific study of human flourishing, and an applied approach to optimal functioning. It has also been defined as the study of the strengths and virtues that enable individuals, communities, and organizations to thrive."

Positive psychology is a relatively new branch within the scientific field of psychology, and it has absolutely exploded. Here's a bit of a history lesson for you. In 1998, Martin Seligman was serving as the president of the American Psychological Association. He had had a change of heart—a change of mindset really—which intensified this emphasis on human flourishing.

Thirty years earlier in his career he had conducted studies where certain dogs were given an electric shock they couldn't escape from. He discovered the conditioning of the dogs caused them to eventually not even try to escape; they had been trained to believe they were unable to change their environments. He coined this condition, "learned helplessness" and found the "giving up" tendencies were similar to people who were diagnosed with clinical depression.

In 1995 his studies took a twist. While weeding the garden with his daughter, Nikki, he became irritated and yelled at her. She got very serious with him and said, "Do you remember that before I was five years old I was a whiner? I whined every day… On my fifth birthday I decided I wasn't going to whine anymore. And that was the hardest thing I have ever done, and I haven't whined since." She looked him in the eye and reasoned with him, "If I can stop whining, you can stop being such a grouch."

Seligman said this was an epiphany for him. His outlook took a twist. His research took a twist. And as the president of the American Psychological Association, he marshaled his forces and encouraged those in his profession to change from focusing on diseases and illnesses—to the science of human flourishing.

For years and years, psychology had been the study of what was wrong with you. Under his leadership they turned their energies towards discovering and replicating what was going right, helping people get in the flow of truly thriving.

Now the University of Pennsylvania has the renowned Positive Psychology Center, UC Berkley has the Greater Good Science Center, Harvard began offering happiness classes (which quickly became the most popular course on campus), and many other top-tier universities offer master's degrees in this exciting new branch of psychology.

Before I go too much further here, let me tell you what positive psychology is not. It's not tricking our brains or fooling ourselves. It's not having a Pollyanna view of life. It's not looking at the world through rose-colored glasses and ignoring all the bad. I can't stress that enough—it certainly is not ignoring the negative and pretending bad stuff doesn't happen. It's the exact opposite. It's about waking up. It's about coming alive. It's about having a greater understanding and awareness of the world around us and then consciously (and that's one of the main key words here) and deliberately choosing to focus on the elements in our lives that will bring greater success. Success in *all* aspects of our lives.

William James, the first educator to offer psychology courses in America, said, "Compared to what we ought to be, we are half awake." So true.

So with this book and the associated online course we're going to help you wake up. You know, come alive. We're going to help you have that greater awareness of the world around you, and then you will have the opportunity to make some choices. You can decide to deliberately focus on what is going right in your life, and, as you do, you will then invite more good things into your life.

Why do good things happen to good people? Why do the rich get richer? When you get in a positive flow, things seem to naturally come together in your favor. It's the optimists' advantage.

METHODOLOGY

The nCOURAGE methodology is simple, yet so powerful.

Education + Deliberate Action + Focused Mindfulness = True Success

The education ... that's what we're doing now. The more you know the more power you have to act. I'll share with you many of the studies conducted through positive psychology. You'll get enlightened with concepts and ideas. I'll point out some obvious things that may seem like common sense but unfortunately are not common practice. And I'll help empower you with trigger words and images so that when you're faced with a choice, you can choose the option that will bring you greater joy, happiness, and success in your life.

Education is the first step to learning to control your mindset.

The Deliberate Action part. This is so awesome. My dear friend, Dr. Christian Laplante, has helped shape this part of our methodology. He's a clinical psychologist with an outrageous French accent. Dr. Laplante has found tremendous success in helping rehabilitate people who have suffered terrible, horrible trauma. He's developed a system, a process for helping these people slowly and methodically overcome their doubts and fears and self-imposed limitations. He does this by giving his patients small, concrete, actionable steps to take.

I remember clearly the first time we sat together and he shared with me some of his success stories. We were outside sitting in a park on a long, cement bench that framed a flower garden. He told me about how some of his patients are often so traumatized that they render themselves completely incapacitated. However, he helps them get into a state of action. He gives them small, extremely clear activities to do. As they do them, they gain confidence in themselves and their abilities and, slowly, little by little, they overcome their fears.

Here's one of the stories he told me that I still remember. He shared with me about a truck driver who had been in a horrific accident. He was so traumatized he was certain he would never drive again. His old life was shattered. Dr. Laplante gave him some homework. He would say, "OK. Today, I want you to go close to your car… I don't want you to touch it… I just want you to go near your car and look at it. I want you to repeat this five times a day." The next activity the man was given was to touch the car. "I don't want you to get in… I just want you to touch the handle. Again, do that for five days and give me a call." The next activity was to get in the car. "I don't want to you to start it up; I just want you to get in. You can listen to the radio if you'd like … maybe put on your favorite station. Do that five times and give me a call." Each activity, each step, got the man further and further back into the life he had known and loved. Eventually, Dr. Laplante got him to drive to his old truck stop and see his buddies, then get into a big rig again, and eventually drive it around. The man is now a truck driver once more and he's earning a solid living for himself and his family.

Small, concrete, actionable steps. That's what we're going to help you do. The more you do them, the more you will get into a growth mindset and eventually into the most successful mindset of all—the deliberate mindset.

So in our methodology we have Education + Deliberate Action + Focused Mindfulness.

You've heard of mindfulness. It's everywhere. You'll hear it in the news. You'll hear about it at work. More and more people are discovering the amazing benefits of intense, deliberate mental focus. Some do this through yoga or meditation, but don't be confused and think that mindfulness is tied to any religion or cultural practice. There are many, many ways to practice mindfulness. The way we will help you do this is through what I call "Practical Mindfulness".

Mindfulness is all about awareness. It's about being intentional about our thoughts. It's all about having a higher level of consciousness. The practical mindfulness in our methodology is so simple—we journal.

Tons of scientific research has confirmed that journaling is one of the most effective interventions you can do to control your mental focus. While it's pretty easy to read through an entire page of something while your mind is wandering, or to listen to a conversation and realize you have no idea what had been said because your mind was off thinking about other things, it's rather hard to think about one thing and write something else. Journaling allows us to be present. To be intentional. It gives us a few minutes to pull in our mental focus on a single task at hand.

When we write things down something changes. And you're going to experience this.

Education + Deliberate Action + Focused Mindfulness. Super simple. So effective. And based on the awesome new research of positive psychology. Exciting, powerful stuff.

— ACTIVITY —

This activity is simple, but you will quickly see how it gives you a chance to—even for only a few minutes—focus on what is going right in your life. First, find a notebook or journal you can use as you go through this book. Then I want you to write a short sentence or two about three people who have made the biggest difference in your life. Write down their names and what about them has inspired you. Ready? Go.

"Gratitude is not only the greatest of virtues,
but the parent of all the others."
— *Cicero*

CHAPTER 6

SKILL #1 – BE GRATEFUL

AS WE JUMP INTO THE 7 CORE SKILLS of Everyday Happiness, we start off with the granddaddy of them all. The skill of gratitude. It's the universal happiness skill.

If you master—and I mean master—only this one skill you can spark your happiness levels whoever and wherever you are, and in whatever circumstances you may find yourself.

Gratitude is the foundational skill. It's the greatest of all the skills of happiness because of this one simple fact: You can't be truly grateful and unhappy any more than you can be both positive and negative at the same time.

Think about that. You can't be truly grateful and unhappy at the same time.

That means if you're feeing unhappy there's something you can do about it. Deliberately, intentionally increasing your gratitude levels will also increase your happiness levels.

When you recognize that gratitude can determine your happiness, you also come to an understanding that your happiness is not determined by your environment or your circumstances. Your happiness is determined by your mindset.

What is gratitude? According to the Greater Good Science Center at UC Berkley, gratitude has two parts. First, it is an affirmation of goodness that we've received. And, secondly, it's recognition that the sources for this goodness are outside ourselves. We acknowledge that other people, or higher powers, gave those gifts.

I like to think of gratitude as recognizing we are the recipients of deliberate kindness.

The *deliberate* part is important because it establishes a connection between us and other people, God, nature, the Universe, or whoever or whatever our benefactor may be. I'll say that again. *Gratitude is recognizing we are the recipients of deliberate kindness.*

Gratitude is different from appreciation. Appreciation is about centering our feelings on an object of goodness. For example, you may appreciate the taste of good meal. Gratitude takes that appreciation to a higher level and recognizes the person who cooked it for you, or the farmer who grew the crops, or the company that organized the shipping, or the host of other people and external forces who worked together to make the tasty meal possible— for you.

Gratitude connects you with others and their deliberate acts of goodness. Gratitude opens the doors to healing. It unlocks opportunities for obtaining additional blessings.

But gratitude does much, much more.

Research cited by the Greater Good Science Center at UC Berkley[8] shows practicing gratitude is one of the most reliable methods for increasing happiness and elevating life satisfaction. It boosts feelings of optimism, joy, pleasure, enthusiasm, and other positive emotions. Gratitude reduces stress, anxiety, and depression. It strengthens our immune systems, lowers our blood pressure, makes us more resilient to illnesses, helps us recover faster, and has been shown to help people bounce back from traumatic events and symptoms including PTSD.

According to a 2001 study by Nancy Digdon[9] published in *Applied psychology: health and Well-being*, subjects who spent 15 minutes every night writing in a gratitude journal experienced longer, sounder sleep. Another study conducted by researchers at the University of Manchester in England[10] studied more than 400 adults (including 40% with sleep disorders) and concluded that gratitude was related to sleeping longer, better, and dozing off quicker.

Gratitude is the characteristic that repeatedly comes up when identifying the traits of uncommonly happy people. Grateful people are happy; it's not the other way around. Gratitude comes first.

What's cool about this is that gratitude is a skill. Sure, some people may be more naturally gifted with gratitude, just as some people are more athletically inclined, but increasing your gratitude levels is simply a matter of deliberately choosing your focus and practicing this repeatedly. Gratitude can be stretched, increased and improved, which in turn increases your natural happiness levels.

Let me tell you a story.

THE DIRTY WELL

I was on a filming trip in Cambodia. We were documenting humanitarian aid to the people in this poor, impoverished country. You may have read the story I told earlier about how transformational this trip was for me because as I traveled around the countryside I saw tons and tons of poor, impoverished people. I saw destitute people but not sad people.

In one small village we were filming an in-progress water well being dug. The villagers were digging the well themselves by hand, and the humanitarian group was paying for the concrete to cement it in and keep it clean. One of the villagers volunteered to climb down this rickety ladder that was no more than a tree branch with a few small boards nailed to it for steps. It never would have held my weight, but this thin, middle-aged man scampered down it with expert agility.

He was down about fifteen feet standing waist-deep in the water using a small shovel to chip away at the edges. We set up the camera directly over the hole and got ready to film. Then the rain came out.

We were drenched. All of the dirt immediately around the hole turned to mud. We got a beautiful shot of the man in the well digging with rain coming down. Then we went to leave.

Here's the cool part.

As we approached our van, a mother and her daughter came carrying a large bucket of fresh, clean water. It was so heavy they had the bucket strung on a rope under a large tree branch, which they each shouldered together. It turns out they brought the fresh water so we could wash our shoes. I was amazed. They were so grateful for the group that was helping them with the well (and they considered us part of that group) that they wanted to show their gratitude by cleaning our shoes with their cleanest, purest water.

Now, I have no idea where the water came from. I had just seen their drinking water. We had stirred up all the mud in that hole for the shot, but they found and donated their cleanest drinking water for our shoes.

It wasn't just pure water. It was pure gratitude.

Gratitude makes for truly happy people.

— ACTIVITY —

Think of something fortunate that happened to you today and write a sentence or two about it. Then I want you to do a bit of a stretch. I want you to think of ANOTHER fortunate thing that happened to you today. This may be a bit harder but you can do it. Then I want you to REALLY STRETCH. I want you to think of a THIRD fortunate thing that happened to you today. And I want you to write it down. This may be one of the most effective habits you can ever train yourself to do.

REFOCUS ON WHAT YOU HAVE

By activating your gratitude you learn to refocus your attention on what you have instead of what you feel you are lacking.

Where's your focus? Are you obsessed with everything you feel you are missing in life? Do you want a new car? A new house? Do you get distracted by "shiny things"? Are you consumed with consumerism? Don't worry; it is easy to do. You're being conditioned to this all the time.

I have a confession to make. I used to be part of this. When I graduated from college I worked as an advertising copywriter. I got skilled at crafting ads so you'd need stuff you didn't really need. I helped train you to buy, buy, buy. My sincere apologies.

There are entire industries that make money off of you spending your money and doing so in a way that doesn't actually satisfy you so you go and spend some more ... and some more...

We get in the squirrel cage of consumerism and start running.

Remember the squirrel cage only stops when we do.

As we discussed in a previous chapter, one of the myths to happiness was telling ourselves the, "I'll be happy when…" lie. Or the misguided belief that happiness is found in things. Or that happiness is found outside of ourselves. Gratitude—deliberate, intentional gratitude—will help us refocus our mindset from obsessing about all the stuff we lack to truly appreciating what we already have.

The simplest, yet most effective, way of activating your skill of gratitude is to write it down. Journal it. Spend time each day recognizing and reflecting on the things you're truly thankful for. I suggest you use the gratitude journal feature in your mobile mindset conditioning program—the Feed Your Happy app. That way, when you're out and about, you can take time to stop and deliberately focus on increasing your gratitude.

Melody Beattie said, "Gratitude unlocks the fullness of life. It turns what we have into enough."

We are constantly being mentally conditioned by society, advertisers, or our circumstances. Decide to take back your focus by being intentional.

Have you ever used a point and shoot camera? It's got this auto-focus feature that seems cool. But then you go to take a photo of something and the camera picks the wrong thing to focus on? Maybe you are taking a picture of your son and this bright orange caterpillar that's crawling on his finger. Somehow, the camera gets it wrong and overshoots the action, focusing on the chain link fence behind your son. When you look at the photo it's a photo of the fence with some weird, blurry blob in the foreground. The camera totally missed what was important and everything gets wildly distorted.

Sometimes we're just like that. *We* miss what's important. We're so busy with our lives and our schedules, our workloads, our various roles and our deadlines. We're so focused on other things that we miss what's important.

Take back your focus. Choose to be mindful. Choose to deliberately take time to feel and express your gratitude.

Part of refocusing is avoiding comparisons.

They say jealousy comes from counting others' blessings instead of our own since we're bound to make accounting errors. Don't focus your energies on what you lack—that's wasted energy. It's like staring at the hole in a doughnut and missing what's all around. Sharpen your skill of truly enjoying what's yours.

Teddy Roosevelt said it best: "Comparison is the thief of joy." So true.

Change your point of view. Consider all the benefits you actually have. Pay special attention to relationships, memories, opportunities, knowledge, health, and other non-material "goods" that can easily get overlooked. This exercise will help you take a deeper dive into your opportunities for genuine, heartfelt gratitude.

— ACTIVITY —

You've got more going for you than you think, or than you're probably thinking right now. Do this: List out everything you have. And I mean everything. Start with the physical things. Hold a garage sale in your mind and write down every item up for grabs. List out all the big stuff then move into the smaller items until you've got everything listed out.

Now consider what your life would be like without them. Will you lose some conveniences or abilities? Are there things that now you consider them you realize they are invaluable treasures? Good stuff, right?

Next, list every talent, ability, opportunity, resource, gift, coincidence, relationship, experience, challenge, and stroke of luck you can think of. Give yourself time to explore these intangibles and the abundant resources you have. There are so many opportunities for sincere, heartfelt gratitude.

Now it's time to move deeper into exploring the assets you can't touch, such as a friend who you could call in the middle of the night for a ride home, or maybe the education that enabled you to read, or the freedom that allow you to live where you live or do what you do.

When you look at life this way, you quickly see you are extremely wealthy. Immensely fortunate. You'll never finish this exercise, but if you start it you'll definitely sharpen your gratitude skills.

RETRAIN YOUR BRAIN TO SEE THE POSITIVE

Robert Emmons, a professor of Psychology at UC Davis, conducted the first major study of gratitude and found "Regular grateful thinking can increase happiness by as much as 25 percent." He outlines the many related benefits from first growing our awareness of the goodness around and then acknowledging those feelings. He distills his research in his book, *Thanks!: How Practicing Gratitude Can Make You Happier.*

Twenty-five percent sounds like something worth working for.

In this lesson we'll talk about how to retrain your brain to see the positive.

We see what we want to see, or, rather, what we're in the habit of seeing. Shawn Achor, in his book, *The Happiness Advantage*, shows that it is possible to train our brains to make positive patterns more automatic. He references Harvard research on the Tetris Effect.

This was a series of experiments where they had students play the game Tetris for prolonged periods of time. If you're unfamiliar with this game, it's a tile-matching video game where the game pieces fall down the playing field while the player works quickly to manipulate the units together to make connections without any gaps.

The study found that that brain continues to make connections even after the game has ended—the Tetris Effect.

Participants' thoughts, mental images, and dreams would envision connections with buildings, books, and boxes of cereal as their minds would have been conditioned to look for those. Achor concludes when we practice looking for more positive aspects of life we can reduce the brain's natural tendency to scan for and spot the negatives.

What can you condition your brain to look for? What patterns would be good for you to see? If you've begun keeping a daily gratitude journal of listing out three fortunate things that happen to you each day, you are on your way to reprogramming your mindset. You are mentally conditioning yourself to focus on what is going right in your life.

The Feed Your Happy app is your mobile mindset conditioning program. Use it to deliberately, consciously participate in activities that have been scientifically shown to increase your happiness levels.

Sometimes our professions or natural tendencies will make us prone to always be looking for the negative. Lawyers have a disadvantage here. They're always looking for loopholes. For problems in contracts. For vulnerabilities and weaknesses. Lawyers are repeatedly conditioned to focus on the negative.

I experienced this myself as a commercial film producer. As I'd prepare for a shoot I would be so consumed with everything that could possibly go wrong. Often I would play the "What if" game. What if the camera goes down … or an actor doesn't show … or a location falls through … or the weather turns bad…

I was so obsessed with everything that hypothetically, might-could-maybe-possibly go wrong that often I failed to recognize what would go right. You know; what magical moments I hadn't anticipated. What actor's performances were waaaay better than the script. What angles the director of photography came up with that just made the scene sing.

There is *always* something good to focus on, but often we don't take the time to stop and recognize it. This is why deliberate mental conditioning is so important.

Regularly writing in a gratitude journal will help you to intentionally train your brain. Sending thank you cards is also quite effective.

A LEGACY OF GRATITUDE

Here's a story. For 23 years, Delmont Oswald was the managing director of the Utah Humanities Council. He held a conference with the governor as he served on his Martin Luther King Jr. Human Rights Commission and other positions. It would be easy for him to feel all too important because of the circles in which he associated. However, Delmont was a man who truly appreciated others.

The first thing he did every morning when arriving to work was to sit at his desk and write thank you cards. "Sending thank you notes was a constant in Delmont's life, as predictable as the sun rising from the east. If someone paid him a compliment or did anything for him or his family, the very next day he would mail a personal note of gratitude," wrote his longtime friend, Frank McEntire, in his eulogy.

When Delmont died, the building was filled to capacity with those wishing to return their thanks for a life well lived. At the funeral Martha Bradley, a co-worker, spoke of how she had just received a card and balloons. She smiled. "He must have sent them while he was in the hospital."

True gratitude, regularly expressed, can condition you to a mindset of abundance.

Ben Stein said, "I cannot tell you anything that, in a few minutes, will tell you how to be rich. But I can tell you how to feel rich, which is far better, let me tell you firsthand, than being rich. Be grateful... It's the only totally reliable get-rich-quick scheme."

— ACTIVITY —

Oprah Winfrey said this: "Be thankful for what you have; you'll end up having more. If you concentrate on what you don't have, you will never, ever have enough."

Think about that. She's right.

With this activity I want you to think about someone who cares about you. Relationships are where we are often waaaaay wealthier than we realize. Take five minutes to write about people in your life who care about you, people who have helped you or who have lifted you. As you write about these people consider why. Why do they care? Why did they help you or lift you?

You, my friend, are an extremely fortunate individual. You're the recipient of deliberate, intentional kindness.

FIND GOOD IN THE BAD

Let's talk about finding good even in the bad—the hallmark trait of the optimist. Again, I pause to remind you that optimism can be trained. You've been training and conditioning yourself already. Keep it up.

So this trait of finding good in the bad, not only is this skill found in uncommonly happy people but it's also a trait identified by those considered resilient—they find the positive side of their challenges and adversity.

This is not to say they hope for challenges, or that they ignore the hard stuff in life or pretend it doesn't exist. But when struggles and difficulty come they look for the lesson. Resilient people turn a negative into a positive by refocusing potentially destructive energy into a force that builds them into something better.

In his bestselling book, *Good to Great*, Jim Collins writes of an interview he had with Jim Stockdale who had survived eight torturous years in a prisoner-of-war camp. "I never lost faith in the end of the story… I never doubted not only that I would get out, but also that I would prevail in the end and turn the experience into the defining event of my life, which, in retrospect, I would not trade."

Stockdale contrasts his successful state of mind with the soldiers who hoped for release by certain dates. After those dates came and went they eventually died of broken hearts.

Stockdale understood his barbaric reality. He didn't pretend it wasn't there. He didn't try to fool his mind or put on rose-colored classes. Stockdale was fully conscious of his terrible reality, but his focus was not on the negative—it was on the outcome. The lesson. What would this teach him? What stories would he have to tell? How would he turn these experiences into the defining moments of his life?

Jim Stockdale chose to focus on what lessons he could learn from his adversity.

Best-selling author Shauna Niequist adds, "When life is sweet, say thank you and celebrate; when life is bitter, say thank you and grow."

Everything good or bad contributes to our advancement. The good stuff can help us grow. And even the bad stuff can help us grow … if we allow it to.

Steve Jobs is celebrated for the advancements he brought to the personal computer and mobile phone industries having created such breakthrough products as the Macintosh, the iPod, the iPhone, and the iPad to name a few. However, many people don't know he was actually fired from the company he helped start. In fact, he was pushed out by the very CEO he hunted down and hired away from Pepsi in order to run his company.

For many that would have been the end of the road, but Steve Jobs allowed the experience to teach him something. When he was given a second opportunity to be a part of Apple Computer, he came back a wiser and much more seasoned businessman. He trained himself to gain the skills necessary to be a CEO—skills he previously lacked.

Being fired from the company he helped start could have defined him. Instead, he turned the experience into his defining moment and rose above it.

It's all in the mindset. I'm sure you know hundreds of other stories of people who looked for the lesson in their unfortunate experiences and it turned out to be the best thing for them.

Be grateful—genuinely, enthusiastically grateful for all of your life lessons.

— ACTIVITY —

Take five minutes and think back to a horrible, terrible incident that happened in your life—something you totally did not want to have happen. Maybe I'm being a bit dramatic here, but that's how we often are when we look at challenging situations. We blow them way out of proportion and lament how hard they've made our lives.

I want you to think back to something that happened in your life that you did not want to have happen. Something in your past that at first seemed like a terrible misfortune. Now I want you to spend five minutes writing about all the good that has come because of it. Think of opportunities you would otherwise have missed that have now come your way. Skills that you now possess that are the direct result. People who have come into your life. Or friends who stepped in and helped you out.

Write about how this experience has, surprisingly, brought much good into your life.

GET RID OF A COMPLAINING HEART

The more you learn about mindsets and the true sources of our happiness the more you realize that what is standing between you and your happiness is … well … you.

I've had people tell me they realize now they have been their own worst enemy. They get "Stinkin' thinkin'" as Zig Ziglar would always say.

Today, let's look at a surefire way to destroy your own happiness—complain.

Jeffrey R. Holland, a former university professor, once said, "No misfortune is so bad that whining about it won't make it worse."

Isn't that so true? Complaining is the polar opposite of expressing gratitude. Where gratitude will bring happiness, peace, and fulfillment, complaining stirs up bitterness, discontentment, aggravation, and annoyance.

Gratitude is about deliberately, consciously choosing to focus on what is going right in your life, and complaining is, well … total, intense focus on the problems with no action involved, presenting no solution, providing no positive alternative options. Complaining is all talk and no action.

What's important to remember is that you have the choice with your mindset. Prepare early. When problems arise it's much harder to slip into the mire of negative thinking if you've been consistently, deliberately finding things to be grateful for.

Get off the negative thinking train. You may have seen our short film called *Falling Up*. It's the true story of Meg Johnson who became a C7 Quadriplegic after a tragic fall from a forty-foot cliff. While the paralysis took much of her mobility away, it couldn't break her spirit. Her discovery of happiness is an inspiration to all. She's one of the most positive people you will ever meet. Having overcome many challenges she is now an inspirational teacher and motivational speaker. After filming, Meg was asked what she missed most about the things she could no longer do. She said, "Oh, if I started to focus on that, where would I stop?"

Meg is smart enough to realize she is in control of her focus.

HERE'S MY STOP

Have your exit strategy ready. When your mind starts to wander down roads that lead to negativity, have a key phrase prepared that you say in your head to remind yourself to switch tracks. "I'm not going there," "Oops, wrong train," or, "I am in charge, and today I choose happiness," are just a few examples. These are the mental triggers we talked about in earlier lessons. Find a trigger that matches your inner voice. Something you can easily remember when your mind starts to barrel down the rails of negativity.

I like to use the phrase, "I'm getting off this train." I can visually see myself jumping off the train and rolling down some grassy hill. It's kind of a funny image for me, so it helps me deliberately take control of my mindset.

THE PROBLEM WITH THANKFULNESS

Now, before we finish up this Core Skill, I want to talk about the problem with thankfulness, or at least a trap you might fall into. You may be like I was when I first read about all the studies on gratitude. *Hey, I'm grateful,* I thought. *I say thank you all the time.* And that was the truth. I would almost always say thank you. It was a habit. An instinct.

I convinced myself that saying thank you was the same as being grateful. It's not.

When I listened to the positive psychology research on the benefits of gratitude I thought this research couldn't be true… *I'm a grateful person—why am I not happy?*

The research says it is impossible to be genuinely grateful and unhappy at the same time. It's like being simultaneously positive and negative—you can't do it.

So why was I not happy? Here I am saying, "Thank you, thank you, thank you…" I would say that to everyone who would do something for me. But it turns out I wasn't feeling gratitude. I was feeling something else. Indebtedness.

Indebtedness is actually bad, bad stuff. It's where, in my case, I felt obligated to thank others for the things they do for me. I felt they were doing things I could not do for myself and it made me feel inferior and that I now had a debt that I could not pay.

Did you catch how I phrased that? I took the victim mindset. I said, "It *made me* feel inferior." Nothing can *make me* anything. I choose how I feel and what I believe. But I took a mindset that turned a positive into a negative. I convinced myself I was being thankful, but deep down I was actually feeling resentful.

Charity workers can often spark feelings of indebtedness in those they serve, which, unfortunately, backfires on their good intentions.

People don't want to feel helpless, poor or powerless. They want to feel valued, important, and that they can make a contribution.

Again, this is a mindset problem. Don't fall into this trap. I go back to the earlier definition: Gratitude is recognizing we are the recipients of deliberate kindness.

Gratitude goes deeper than recognizing an exchange of kindness. Gratitude explores the why behind it—

- Why did my wife make me this sandwich? *Oh, it's because she loves me.*
- Why did that man hold the elevator door open for me? *Oh, it's because we're part of the same human family.*
- Why did my friend let me use his truck to move a broken washer? *It's because he is my friend. My true friend.*

Gratitude is deeper than a thank you. Gratitude is recognizing and savoring the good intention behind the kindness. Gratitude connects us to the human family. We're not isolated. We're connected.

Eckhart Tolle said, "Acknowledging the good that you already have in your life is the foundation for all abundance."

Also, gratitude takes a bit of humility because we have to allow ourselves to "receive".

Some say it's better to give than receive. Sometimes it's easier too. Receiving can be difficult when we've been conditioned to be independent, "I can do it myself," sort of people.

One way to handle this is not to look at the exchange as a physical thing (for example, someone buys your lunch, gives you a gift, or even pays you a compliment). Instead of looking at it as a physical exchange look at it as an exchange of love. This is done by remembering the "why".

We are the recipients of deliberate kindness. Intentional love.

— ACTIVITY —

Take five minutes and think about someone who has in the past (day, year or decade) done something kind for you. Maybe you haven't thanked them properly. You haven't forgotten them or their act of kindness, it's stuck with you. Now that you're thinking about their intentions, your gratitude levels deepen and you are ready to write them a letter of gratitude.

Take a few minutes and write the letter. Don't worry if you feel the incident was too far in the past to thank them; that can actually be a good thing. It means you've been thinking about them a long time. It made that much of an impact on you. Ready? Go.

"Happiness will never come to those who don't appreciate what they already have."
— *Unknown*

CHAPTER 7
SKILL #2 – SAVOR THE NOW

CONGRATULATIONS. YOU'VE MADE IT TO THE SECOND Core Skill of Everyday Happiness. I hope you're taking the time to soak in each lesson and concept. I hope you're doing the work to turn these ideas into actions, the actions into habits and the habits into a lifestyle.

I hope you enjoyed the Core Skill on gratitude. That is such a transformational skill. How amazing that we can spark our happiness whenever and wherever we are simply by actively, deliberately focusing on our gratitude, on our recognition that we are the recipients of intentional kindness, and that there's deeper meaning behind the intentional kindness.

I hope your life is already starting to spiral up. As you've participated in the activities, I hope you've recognized the feelings they stir inside. In doing a ton of research to create this book, I have been surprised to hear repeatedly that when we write things down, when we go over in our heads the experiences we've had, we actually re-live them. Our brains can't tell the difference between the actual positive experience we've just created in our lives and the memory as we re-live them and write them down.

There have been a number of studies on athletes who take time to visualize out their game or their event and the researchers will find various muscles being triggered and activated simply through the visualization or the memory. So when you're participating in the nCOURAGE methodology of education

+ deliberate action + focused mindfulness, you're repeatedly conditioning your brain to focus on what's going right in your life and you're training your mind to look for and expect good things to happen.

Before we jump into the heart of Skill #2, I want to take a moment to visualize with you. We've talked about this before, the importance of visualization. You never create a film without visualizing it out first, why would we live our lives without doing the same? Most importantly, why would we go through this whole mindset conditioning experience without picturing clearly in our minds how our lives will be different—how our lives will be better—once we complete the training? It would be awesome to storyboard this out. For now, let's create some mental pictures in our heads.

Remember we're doing mindset conditioning here; we're training ourselves to have the mindset of the optimist. Think of the most optimistic person you know. Picture their face in your mind. See if you can visualize their smile. Listen in your mind to hear their laugh. You are striving to have that kind of peace and joy and contentment in your life. This is where you are headed.

Now imagine, if you will, that you've gone through this whole book and you've learned all seven Core Skills of Everyday Happiness. Imagine what those skills will do for you and your relationships. Picture yourself with friends and loved ones laughing and smiling. Visualize how people seem to be drawn to you; you convey this feeling of peace and contentment. Imagine yourself being successful at work. Your self-confidence has grown as you're now fully conscious of all the good in your life. Stress, anxiety, and worry don't seem to faze you. You've found a sense of purpose and meaning in your life. And at the end of each night you go to bed with a smile on your face, grateful for your happy and fortunate life.

This process of visualization is super effective. It's the same process used by top performing athletes before a competition. As I mentioned, it's the process for creating any quality film or inspiring work of art.

Napoleon Hill who famously wrote, "Anything the mind can conceive and believe, it can achieve," also penned another quote of which you might want to take notice. He said, "If you want the mind to pick up an idea and to form a habit so that the mind will automatically act upon that idea, you've got to tell the mind what you want, over and over and over again."

Repeated visualization will help you achieve that.

THE ART OF SAVORING

Now let's jump into Skill #2 – SAVOR THE NOW. We've talked about how happiness is a skill—it's actually a set of skills and each of the skills has a smattering of sub-skills. SAVOR THE NOW can mean being present. It can mean enjoying what you have. It can mean not delaying happiness. It can mean pausing to reflect and enjoy. It can mean finding a zest for life again. It can mean not worrying about the future.

All of these are deliberate mindsets you can get into, which will increase your happiness levels.

So what does it mean to savor?

I like to think of it as doing all that you can to make the experience last as long as possible.

Think about what you savor or like to savor. Food immediately comes to mind. Maybe there's a taste that you love to have linger on your tongue as long as possible. You bite into a goldenly ripe peach and it's just dripping with juice. As you take a bite it squirts out and gets all over your hands and even down your arm a bit. You love every bite, with the sweet, juicy goodness. Your mouth is watering just thinking about it, right? You want this to last as long as possible. And what do you do when the peach is all done? You lick your fingers, *Mmmmm*, hoping to get every last drop.

In a nutshell, that's the art of savoring. Making positive experiences last as long as humanly possible.

I'm afraid to tell you that society has not been conditioning you to savor anything. Advertisers try to get you to buy the next latest and greatest shiny thing and as soon as you buy it, they want you to move on to the next, and the next, and the next.

Our lives are so busy we don't take time to stop and even notice beautiful moments, let alone savor them.

We're conditioned to live life in the fast food lane. We don't mindfully eat; we hork it down.

Sadly, relationships also don't get savored like they could be where we enjoy them to their fullest.

SAVOR THE NOW—the art of relishing, appreciating, and enjoying life, love, moments, memories, music, relationships, opportunities, sights, smells, experiences—everything good in our lives—that is an art. That is a skill worth mastering.

— ACTIVITY —

Do this. Stop what you're doing right now and look at something you've taken for granted. I'll give you a moment. Look around for something that's become commonplace in your life; something that you don't think much about but that actually provides a ton of value to you.

Think what everyday life would be like without it. How it has blessed or enriched you. Think of the time it took to design it and create it. Think of the person responsible for its existence. Imagine the work he or she must have put in to come up with the idea and see it to fruition. Picture in your mind the manufacturing process. See how many people may have been involved in making this item.

Now think about the distribution channels. There was likely shipping. There was likely a store and an inventory system. Think about all of the effort that was put in to bring just this one item to you.

Life is good, right? Take a few minutes to write about your thoughts and experiences with this activity.

ENJOY WHAT YOU HAVE

We're going to talk about getting maximum enjoyment out of everything we can possibly savor (life, love, relationships, opportunities … really anything good in life). This is about being more alive, more awake, more conscious. Again, the key to accomplishing this is to do it deliberately.

We've talked about gratitude and how it's different from appreciation. Gratitude is where your focus or emphasis is on the kindness of your benefactor in bestowing a deliberate gift of kindness on you. Appreciation is different, and truly is at the heart of the SAVOR THE NOW skill set.

Appreciation is about focusing on the gift. Gratitude is being conscious of the giver. Both are important and vital to our happiness.

Appreciation takes both time and thought. It's a conscious, deliberate act of recognizing and evaluating positive aspects of your life. It's enjoying the sun on your face, the cool breeze in the summer or the sound of your friend's voice. Find moments to pause and reflect. Enjoy. Savor. Relish. Admire.

It's so easy to get trapped in the squirrel cage of out-of-reach happiness. "I'll be happy when..." is a phrase that can be punctuated with limitless possibilities. Yet rarely is it ever true. Generally, if we reach that goal we find it empty of the expected happiness and we then rephrase it with a new goal. And so on. And so forth. Happiness with this approach is always a carrot stick away. But if you learn the skill of enjoying what you have right now—really savoring it—you'll find enjoyment and satisfaction is not only within your reach, it's actually in your hands.

Part of SAVOR THE NOW is enjoying what you have right now. It's about stopping to notice and appreciate it. I know this sounds bonehead-obvious, but it's amazing how often we miss this.

Let's take food for example.

Do you believe food makes you happy? Good food? Tasty food? That's what I used to believe before I took a good, long look at how I "appreciated" food ... with two fists ... knife and fork ready. I would shovel the food in. Excitedly.

With a mouth full of food, I'd be scoping out my next bite. *Ooh, that one's going to make me happy.* And as soon as I had that bite in my mouth I was on to the next bite because that one had sauce! *Yeah,* that's *going to make me happy.* As I'm shoveling that bite in, I look at the serving bowl or plate and realize if I hurry not only can I eat what's on my plate, but I can get the extras before everyone else.

I devoured food. Are you like this? Think about your approach to mealtime or snack time.

Also, did you catch the myth of happiness I used to believe? That food would *make me* happy? It can't make me anything—I have to choose it.

When I started thinking about how I approached food I realized I never savored my food. In fact, I really didn't even taste it. Each time I had a bite in my mouth my concentration was actually on the *next* bite. How can you enjoy what you're chewing if you're completely focused on what's next?

This is true in savoring life, just as it's true in savoring food. Unless we deliberately pause to enjoy what we've got, we miss out on pure pleasure. As Ferris Bueller, the poet Laureate of '80s teen movies, repeatedly said, "Life moves pretty fast. If you don't stop and look around once in a while, you could miss it."

I do want to point out that when I realized how I was approaching food I realized I ate totally out of habit—never intention. The only way I knew if I was satisfied was if I felt bloated. Completely stuffed. When I started eating mindfully—in other words I started paying attention to what I was doing—I ate slowly. I savored each and every bite. I employed a few strategies like deliberately putting my knife and fork down while I was chewing so I wouldn't automatically move on to the next bite. When I started doing this, not only did I start truly enjoying my food but I also lost 20 pounds!

Learn to SAVOR THE NOW. Learn to savor what you have right now.

If you're like me you've been caught in those myths of happiness. You know, the "I'll be happy when…" myth or the lie that "[fill in the blank] will *make me* happy." Learning to appreciate—truly, deliberately appreciate what you have right now—will put you back in control of your happiness.

One way you can do this is to stop looking.

When you find something good, enjoy it. Don't always go looking for something better or something else. Call off the search. Be content with what you have.

Dan Gilbert, a Harvard psychologist, in a 2002 study titled "Decisions and Revisions: The Affective Forecasting of Changeable Outcomes"[11] found that, although people prefer to make changeable decisions rather than unchangeable ones, people who had the opportunity to change their minds after making a decision liked their original choice less than those who were not given the opportunity to change.

The study was super interesting. People were given options for a piece of art they could keep. Some were given the opportunity to "have second thoughts" and change their decision, while another group was not given that option. The group who made their choice and moved on were much happier with their artwork than were those given the chance to second-guess themselves.

Choices, although generally preferred, made us miserable. This is a twist to the 1956 Brehm experiment known as the "free-choice paradigm", which has been replicated numerous times.

The point is the quicker we can move from the decision-making process to the enjoyment phase the happier we will be. And not only that, but if we are conscious and deliberate about savoring and appreciating what we have, we find happiness all around us.

– ACTIVITY –

Sometimes we're so focused on what we want that we forget about everything we already have. Refocus your brain. Right now let's look at the things you already have. Grab a pen and some paper and start writing them down. Some will come quickly to mind. That's the easy stuff. I want you to then dig deeper. Don't just think of stuff. Think of relationships. Opportunities. Conveniences. Think of the skills and talents you've got. Think of technologies and maybe your ability to use those technologies. Think of your challenges and setbacks—what good things are they bringing you? List as many out as you possibly can for a few minutes.

Part of SAVOR THE NOW is enjoying what you have right now. It's about stopping to notice and appreciate it. Again I point out that we often think this concept is bonehead-obvious, but it's amazing how often we miss it. Common sense is not always common practice.

Condition your mind to look for and appreciate the good stuff you already have in your life. Now savor it.

EVERYDAY MIRACLES

An important part of this skill is learning to savor the moment. First off, let me tell you a story. It's about "everyday miracles".

Several years ago I was on a filming trip in Ecuador. The producer, Tyler, and I arrived a few days before the rest of the film crew and we decided to meet some of the people to see who would be good candidates for the documentary once the crew arrived.

I don't speak much Spanish, so Tyler led out. He would talk with each person, get a sense of their story, and then let me know if he thought they'd be good to film.

While he talked, I'd listen. I was looking for more of a gut feeling on whether I thought the person was honest and sincere. The film was for church people and I know what resonates with that sort of audience, so I was looking for something that connects on a spiritual level.

Near the end of nearly every conversation, Tyler's eyebrows would shoot up as he'd ask, "Meercoles?" They'd respond back, "Si, si Miéroles."

Each house in the neighborhood was the same. Tyler would talk, he'd look over at me and nod then he'd question them further. "Meercoles?" They would repeat back, "Si, si Miércoles."

I was excited. Every house had a miracle story. This film was going to be fun and would totally connect with the audience.

As we walked to yet another house I asked Tyler, "So tell me about these miracles." Tyler looked confused. "Meercoles, meercoles, everyone keeps saying meercoles. What are the miracle stories?"

Tyler smiled, "Miéroles means Wednesday. I told them we'd be back to film on Wednesday."

I've thought a lot about that story over the years. I come looking for miracles and what I find is Wednesday. Which is perfect. What could be more ordinary than Wednesday? It's not Monday, it's not the start of something. It's not Friday and the anticipation that day brings. No, it's the most common, ordinary day of the week.

If you're looking for miracles you'll find them. They key is: you need to be looking for them.

For me now Wednesday means miracles. I've trained myself to look for them, to anticipate and expect them. Often, I find them in the most average, everyday experiences. Tender mercies disguised as tiny, beautiful moments. Then each night I write about them in my gratitude journal.

It has made all the difference as I've learned to savor the moment—each and every moment—and appreciate the true gift that is the present.

SAVOR THE MOMENT

Hopefully that gives you a sense of how to savor the moment. Like food, sometimes we're focused too much on what's coming or what's next to truly enjoy what we have. We hork it down without taking the time to savor each bite or we run from activity to activity without taking time to pause and reflect.

Life can be hectic, even chaotic at times. There are so many opportunities to be busy, busy, busy with work, education, entertainment, and socializing agendas that we're constantly on the run.

But if we're always racing to the next moment, what happens to the one we're in? Carpe diem is a Latin adage usually translated to "seize the day." This can be interpreted to mean many things not the least of which is to train yourself not to let the day go by without recognizing the greatness and beauty around.

I hope you're using your Feed Your Happy app. It's your mobile mindset conditioning tool. Use the reminder system to deliberately schedule your workouts. Also, you can tap into the journal section for daily prompts that will help you focus on what is going right in your life.

Looking to savor the moment right now? Try this: Be amazed again. Why is it that children are so happy? Think of the discovery and newness of life they enjoy. You've felt it too, but familiarity dulls our senses.

Rejuvenate that excitement by looking at something old with fresh eyes again, or by getting out of the comfort zone of routine and experiencing the joy of discovery that comes with cultivating new talents, expanding education, or plotting new adventures. Allow yourself to attempt new things. Scary things. Uncomfortable things. Things that make you go, "Wow."

Find joy in the ordinary. One way to enjoy what you already have is to discover what is so common, so familiar, so everyday we miss it. The old adage stop and smell the roses provides timeless counsel.

Savor your everyday miracles.

— ACTIVITY —

Don't just do something, stand there.

This may sound counterintuitive to everything you've been taught—and likely practiced—but sometimes the best thing to do is to just stop. Completely stop. And do nothing but become aware.

Take a look at what's around you, both natural and man-made. Consider what led you to be where you are right now, today. Notice the building or landscape around and what the fine details reveal. Reflect on the human interactions you've enjoyed. Breathe in the air. Find the beauty. Sometimes you have to come to a complete stop in order to see all you've got going for you.

Take a few minutes and write about your experience.

BE ALL THERE

Jim Elliot said, "Wherever you are, be all there."

Have you ever been so preoccupied with something that you missed what was going on right in front of you? This happens frequently with parents who are so consumed with video taping their child's school performance that they are actually watching their child through the tiny three-inch monitor.

They're there but not really there. They're missing the beauty of life.

You've had conversations with these types of people too, right? Sure, they're in the same room with you physically, but sometimes they're not even on the same planet.

I find this happens when I read sometimes. My mind could be wandering on some problem somewhere and when I go to turn the page I realize I have no idea what I just read.

Does this happen to you? Can you read something or be "listening" to some conversation and realize when you "wake up" that you have no idea what's just been said?

It takes deliberate, conscious effort to block out other thoughts and distractions and stay in the moment.

William Feather once said, "Plenty of people miss their share of happiness, not because they never found it, but because they didn't stop to enjoy it."

Take time to relish the moment. Remove distractions. Empty your mind of thoughts that can take you away.

Make a plan for yourself to give people your full attention. Don't have your smartphone out between you and them. Don't be thinking about tomorrow's schedule. Enjoy. Savor. Relish who you're with.

If schedules and to-do items keep you preoccupied, make it a habit to keep a notecard on hand on which you can quickly jot down a thought or idea— then jump right back into being present.

Mindfulness is about enjoying a deeper sense of awareness of the world around you. It's about deliberately, consciously choosing what to focus on. It's about learning to live in what's happening.

WHAT CAN YOU FEEL?

Here's an interesting thought. Take a deep breath. Breathe it in through your nose and fill up your lungs. Now put your hand on your chest. Can you feel that? Feel that pounding? Can you feel this sense that your heart and lungs are pushing, pushing, pushing clean, oxygenated blood through your body from right here?

Take another deep breath in through your nose. See if you can totally fill up your lungs. You feel your chest expanding. Maybe you smell some things around you. The point is the feelings you're feeling right now. Your breath, your heartbeat, the sensitivity you get with your fingertips, they can only be felt right now.

The present, it is a gift. This moment we're in together, the feelings we have, the opportunities to go and do, it only happens right now.

Filmmaking—I think I've mentioned this to you before—is all about the present. Even if you're filming a period piece, meaning it's a story set back in history, or even if you're doing some futuristic scene, it can only be filmed in the present.

The scripts are all written in present tense. "The man opens the door slowly … there's a creak as the large, wooden door swings to reveal…"

When you're actually filming, you can only film in the present. You can only press record on the audio right now, not five minutes ago—that time is lost. You and I can't start rolling film on what is going to happen in five minutes.

As a filmmaker, the only time you have to create, to make a piece of art or capture a beautiful scene—the only time you can do that is right now.

So why do we tend to live everywhere but where we are right now? We're worried about what happened five minutes or five days ago. We're stressed about what's maybe-might-possibly going to happen two weeks or two years from now.

"Wherever you are be all there." Learn to live in the present. Condition your mind to SAVOR THE NOW. This moment you have—right here—right now, this is the moment you have to create a life of purpose and meaning.

Junia Bretas, a motivational speaker from Brazil, has wisely pointed out:
"If you are depressed you are living in the past.
If you are anxious you are living in the future
If you are at peace you are living in the present."

Train your brain to be truly present.

THE SKILL OF ANTICIPATION

Now we're going to talk about using the skill of anticipation. You might think anticipation runs counter to being in the moment. We're going to talk about how to use it to our advantage.

First a story.

One of my daughters has always been extremely advanced. The day before one of her birthdays, she announced, "In a day and a year—I'll be four!" I was amazed at the math skills she was able to grasp at such an early age, but also a bit unsettled that she might be developing a habit of wishing her life away.

Anticipation can easily make us slip into an "I'll be happy when…" mode, which keeps happiness always a carrot stick away.

The key for using the skill of anticipation in order to SAVOR THE NOW is simply to do it deliberately. Mindfully. Intentionally. In other words, you don't let anticipation delay your happiness for some future event; you use anticipation to bring happiness. You deliberately invite pleasant thoughts of future events then use those thoughts to savor the good feelings they've brought.

For instance, you may have a wonderful vacation coming up. Maybe you're going to Hawaii. That's going to be fantastic. Well, it already is if you use it right. Take a few moments to envision yourself walking on the beach, the soft breeze blowing in your hair. The waves crash as children laugh in the distance. You can almost taste the saltiness in the air as a gentle, warm breeze blows a mist of ocean spray against your cheek. Oh, there's a hint of tropical plumeria flowers that smells so good. *Mmmm. This is awesome.*

Now disengage from the future and savor how you feel right now. Oh, this feels great! How fortunate that you get to go on this trip. How amazing that your life is so blessed.

Anticipation. It's an awesome tool that you can deliberately engage to spark your happiness.

And if you think about it, you can use the same principle with memories in your past.

Don't live in the past. Don't let them consume you, that life was somehow better back then, but use them to savor a memory. Relish it. Drink it in. Then smile as you realize how good you feel right now.

Memories are awesome tools for helping us refocus on the relationships that make our lives worth living.

On my smartphone, I like to keep a list of fortunate things that have happened to me. I can revisit the list anytime and spark up my happiness almost immediately.

Hopefully, you've been using the Feed Your Happy app. This is your Mobile Mindset Conditioning System. In either the Journal section or the Knowledge Base section, you can go back and revisit and remember the good experiences you've intentionally created.

Deliberately using the skills of remembering or intentionally anticipating the thoughts of your choosing are awesome tools for controlling your mindset and enjoying the present.

Before we leave this lesson, there's one more concept that's important to understand.

Take time to relax. They say, "Never get so busy making a living that you forget to make a life." One strategy to enjoying the now is to take time to relax and unwind. Stephen Covey lists this as his seventh principle of highly effective people and calls it "Sharpening the saw." Find time each day to refuel. However, don't confuse relaxing with a state of doing nothing.

The best way to re-energize yourself is through pursuits. Find activities that bring you peace, enjoyment, or give you a rush of excitement—that's how you refuel. You do activities that bring back the energy of your life.

Rabbi Harold Kushner said, "Nobody on their deathbed ever says they wish they had spent more time at work." Spend time with family. FOSTER POSITIVE RELATIONSHIPS. Engage in noble pursuits.

You have the power to choose your mindset and amplify your happiness.

— ACTIVITY —

As we talked about the Hawaii trip, did it conjure up images in your mind of an upcoming trip or event in your life? Whether it did or not, I want you to spend a few minutes thinking about something you have coming up to look forward to. Picture it in your mind. Visualize what it will look like. What will you be wearing? What will the temperature be like? How does it smell? Is there a taste associated with it?

Now spend a few minutes writing about your upcoming, highly anticipated activity. Now don't forget this part—this is super important. Make sure you also write about how you feel right now as you envision yourself engaging in this activity. Write about how fortunate you are right now to be you and to have these awesome opportunities.

FORGIVING OTHERS

Here's a sure-fire way to upskill your happiness, and it's probably one you may have overlooked—forgiveness.

Think about it. How can you possibly be "in the moment" if your mind is consumed with obsessing over grievances in the past?

Part of SAVOR THE NOW is getting rid of the bitter aftertaste of yesterday. Letting it go. Allowing ourselves to move on.

When I started studying research in positive psychology, I was surprised at all the research about forgiveness. I thought that it was a religious concept. But for the last twenty years social scientists have been conducting empirical research validating the connections between forgiving others and overall personal health and well-being.

The benefits are amazing. Researchers find that "forgiving people" have fewer episodes of depression, higher self-esteem, better social skills, more friends, lower blood pressure, better immune systems, and lower rates of heart disease.

Forgiveness is a choice. It's not about condoning, excusing, or brushing past grievances aside. It's about recognizing them, and then extending compassion even—maybe more especially—when that compassion is undeserved.

Here's a story.

After the brutal murder of his mother, psychologist Everett L. Worthington, Jr. dedicated his career to the study of forgiveness. Among the many findings are connections between forgiveness and physical, mental, and spiritual health as well as invoking positive repercussions on relationships in families, communities, and nations. Worthington wrote about his experiences in his book, *Forgiving and Reconciling: Bridges to Wholeness and Hope.*

As he traveled his personal journey to wholeness, he would often ask himself, "In this instance, should I forgive?" Then he candidly weighed the pros and cons of each option. What he found through reflection is insightful.

He defines forgiveness as "reducing or eliminating resentment and motivations toward revenge."

I'll say that again. *Forgiveness is about reducing or eliminating resentment and motivations toward revenge.*

Release the negative energy and let it go. Purge yourself of toxic emotions. It doesn't matter if the person who harmed you is apologetic, remorseful, or deserving of your forgiveness. It's actually not about them. It's about you— you deserve it. It's your happiness that's at stake here, not theirs.

Remember nothing you can do right now can change your past, but it will most definitely affect your future.

We can all come up with reasons why a certain person does not deserve our forgiveness. This is a trap. Don't let your mind take you there. Forgiveness is not about them … it's about you. I can't stress this enough.

I was conducting a workshop once and was sharing a bit about the science of forgiveness when a woman started telling me about some horrible, terrible incident that she went through with her ex-husband and immediately tried getting the rest of the room to back her on this. She wanted to prove she had a reason to hate him, to hold these grudges and to withhold forgiveness. She was so bitter and you could see it in her face.

She wasn't withholding any healing balm for him, she was, as they say, "Drinking poison and hoping the other person would die."

While the physical damage occurred many years before, she was keeping the pain fresh and close to her heart by reliving the past. She transformed physical pain into emotional baggage. She was perpetually recirculating the bitter poison of anger and vengeance, and the poison's effects were clearly seen in her face. It was tragic really.

We all have people who have hurt us. Don't fall into the trap of living in the past. Don't get stuck obsessing over something so obviously negative in your life. Get rid of the toxic emotions of yesterday. Enjoy the now. SAVOR THE NOW.

Akshay Dubey surmised this well by saying, "Healing doesn't mean the damage never existed. It means the damage no longer controls our lives."

Allow yourself to heal. Live in the now. Savor life. This is a skill that takes time and perseverance. Keep striving. Keep forgiving.

One last note: Part of forgiving others is forgiving ourselves. Sometimes we beat ourselves up for mistakes we've made in the past. It's an easy thing to do; hindsight is always 20/20. But nothing you can do right now will change the past so don't worry about it. Learn the lesson and move on.

Successful people aren't focused on what went on in their past because they're too busy creating their future. Study the science of forgiveness and learn about the physical, social, and mental health benefits that come even—and maybe more importantly—if the person you need to forgive is you.

Here's an inspiring quote from Mandy Hale: "Forget the past. Remember the lesson."

— ACTIVITY —

Find someone to forgive. Think of an incident in the past that's holding you back. Don't let a grudge that's focused on a misfortunate historical event prevent you from enjoying happiness now. Choose to relieve yourself from the mental toxin of a grudge by learning to just "let it go".

Yes, this is a skill. And, yes, this can be a challenging skill to master.

Have you thought of someone against whom you're holding a grudge? Here's an exercise that will help you visualize yourself letting go of the past. Take a deep breath and imagine the incident getting sucked into an open book the way a genie must return to his lamp. The book closes. This is a chapter of your life that is now closed; you're ready to move on. Picture the book transforming into a beautiful, majestic bird that then opens her wings and flies gracefully away into the distance.

The past is past. You are here now, safe, where the pain of memory can no longer hurt you.

Now, as you go through this exercise, pay attention to how you feel. Recognize the weight that gets lifted from your shoulders. The deeper you're able to breathe. The stress that seems to melt away.

You did that. Your conscious, deliberate choice just changed both your mental and physical state.

Don't forget to journal this.

Now that you recognize grudges are choices, the next time you slip into the stressful, anxious, resentful conditions again you will remember you know how to rid yourself of these toxic emotions. You've practiced the skill of removing negative energy from your body and you've felt the relief and clarity that comes with genuine forgiveness.

TAKE TIME TO MOURN

Today, we're going share together about an extremely important skill to happiness—mourning.

Sadness. The feelings of loss and disappointment … these are healthy, healthy feelings. These are the emotions we have inside when our hearts break or when we help others whose hearts are currently breaking. These are good feelings. Allow yourself to feel the heartache of loss and sadness.

Don't be embarrassed. Crying is healthy. Cathartic. Don't rush to get it *out of your system*. Feeling emotion, feeling deep tenderness or connectedness with others is a wonderful, beautiful experience. Savor it.

Not the pain. Don't focus on the pain. Concentrate on what the pain *means*. It means that you're human. That you love. That you care about others. You have compassion.

Yes, there are vulnerabilities as you experience these emotions but, again, these are good things. It's too easy in society to get hardened, to feel nothing, But that's not the essence of life. That's not being fully awake. That's not what vitality is about.

Allow yourself to feel more alive. Allow yourself to experience this connection with others as your heart aches and breaks.

Many people struggle for years with issues because they didn't allow themselves time to genuinely grieve. They wrestle with guilt and shame. They didn't allow themselves to find a purpose in the pain.

Viktor Frankl, the author of *Man's Search for Meaning,* when talking about his experiences in a Nazi concentration camp, said, "There was no need to be ashamed of tears, for tears bore witness that a man had the greatest of courage, the courage to suffer." He then went on to say, "If there is meaning in life at all then there must be meaning in suffering."

Find your meaning in your suffering, in the pain and heartache you experience. Then—and this is super important—once you feel you have learned what it is you had to learn from the experience (again, this is not focused on the pain or even the cause of the pain but the MEANING behind the pain), once you have embraced the revelation that you deeply care about and love others, then allow yourself to be freely happy again. To laugh and to love again. To trust. Allow yourself to be vulnerable through love once more.

I hope this makes sense to you. In this mindset conditioning training, I want you to experience everything you can that will make you feel more awake and alive. I want you to be more conscious. I want you to enjoy love and happiness. Pain and grief are part of that. The key to remember is to be in control of your mindset. Just like rushing through grief just to "get it out of our system" will cheat you of opportunities to experience love and connectedness, you also don't want to be defined by sadness. You don't want it to control you any more than you would allow outside influences to control your happiness. As they say, "Don't put the keys to your happiness in someone else's pocket."

A healthy mental state is an expressive mental state. Mourning is part of that.

Nicholas Sparks, in his novel, *A Walk to Remember*, said, "There are moments when I wish I could roll back the clock and take all the sadness away, but I have a feeling that if I did, the joy would be gone as well."

Part of SAVOR THE NOW is allowing ourselves to feel those deep emotions that bring the spice of life, that awaken our sense of compassion. To feel is to love. Savor love.

– ACTIVITY –

Practice feeling emotions. Today, I want you to listen to three of your favorite songs with your eyes closed. Ruminate on the flood of memories, the sights, the smells, the memories the songs bring to you. As you listen to your music, focus on your feelings. Let the music stir your soul, and then write about how you feel in your journal.

STOP MULTITASKING

Society tells us we should be multitaskers, yet as we divide our attention among several pursuits we limit our ability to focus. People thought (and unfortunately some still do) that multitasking was a way to be more efficient. After all you're working on several things at once, more's bound to get accomplished, right? According to some studies though, multitasking can reduce productivity by as much as 40 percent.[12]

Take back your focus. As you concentrate your energies with laser-like precision on a single activity, you're able to enjoy the flow that comes with being totally immersed in an endeavor.

Are you living intentionally? The goal of this training is to empower you to be more in control. To enjoy the peace and freedom that comes from living a life true to ourselves. To find the satisfaction that comes from inner harmony. To be at one with ourselves and the world around us.

Multitasking makes one-ness impossible.

As you participate in the journaling activities in this book and in the Feed Your Happy mobile mindset conditioning app, you are providing yourself opportunities to—for a few minutes—completely focus on one task at hand. And all of it is wholly focused on improving your happiness levels.

Now consider this. How many hours of the day are you most effective? Ten? You're totally, completely effective for ten hours a day? OK, I didn't think so. How 'bout eight? Six? Are you completely, 100% effective for six hours? Turns out, most people say two. They have two hours each day when they're most effective, when they're at their peak.

So what are you doing with your two hours? When are they? Are they in the morning? Do you get your best work done bright and early in the morning before all the distractions take over? Are they in the evening? Are you an owl? Is that when you find yourself most creative or when you are the sharpest?

Whenever your two or your four hours of peak performance are, are you living intentionally here? Do you block out this time so you're not distracted by e-mails or phone calls, or do you juggle all the distractions as you normally do during the rest of the day?

Are you doing anything intentional to protect your peak time—the time you recognize you're usually the most alert and alive? Be more successful; stack the deck in your favor. Deliberately, consciously create your environment (which also means eliminate and edit out the distractions) so your peak time can be your most productive.

See how much more effective you can be when you're focused on one thing? When you intentionally create harmony within yourself that you're living in accordance with what will make you most successful.

There are so many different ways you can learn to take back your mental focus. So many things you can do to condition yourself so you realize you always have choice. You're not a victim of your circumstances or held down by your environment. You are free to choose your attitude.

Success comes from the deliberate mindset.

– ACTIVITY –

Let's start out easy. For the next twenty minutes, strive to completely focus on one task. Don't let texts or e-mail alerts distract you (in fact, you might want to turn them off). Allow yourself to get completely immersed in a single task. Get into a state of flow. This is where you're in the zone. You're feeling it. Things are clicking.

Spend twenty minutes giving your whole attention to one thing then come back here and write about it.

Ready? Go.

THE YAGOTTAWANNA PRINCIPLE

Scientists have found intrinsic motivations are directly linked to our happiness levels.

When we allow our motivations to be determined extrinsically, in other words we feel pushed or coerced to do something, once meaningful activities can feel less enjoyable and gratifying.

Remove the phrase, "I have to," from your life, it devalues the activity and implies you are no longer in charge of choosing but are victimized by an obligation.

You are not a victim of your circumstances. You are an agent of choice. Simply put: You don't have to "do" anything. If you apply the Yagottawanna principle, you get to.

Now, to enjoy this mindset, you must make it your choice. This can be challenging when faced with unpleasant activities that, on the surface, you might not have initially chosen. Maybe there's a dinner date with the in-laws, a tedious 3rd quarter sales analysis due, or a service call with an unpleasant client. Make it a game to find your intrinsic or inner motivations. The more distasteful the activity the greater the opportunity to turn a negative into a positive. You're up to the challenge.

Let me also share with you how to remove negative speak from your life. You shouldn't ever say, "should."

This is when you tell yourself, "Well, I *should* clean up the room," or, "I *should* take care of the dishes," or, "I *should* help out at that service project."

These are all wonderful things. Things that will likely improve your life and the lives of others. The problem comes in how we think about them.

When we say the word "should," we are taking our motivations and making them external. And when we do that, we are doing it for someone else, or out of duty, or for the appearance of looking better or properly conforming.

An unknown author said, "If you do something out of duty it will deplete you but if you do something out of love it will energize you." Wise counsel.

Doing things—even good things—out of duty does not lead to happiness. It makes you feel you are a slave or encumbered, or that you're being forced to do things. Live a life of choice.

Make all of your choices internal. Make them things you want to do or that you've decided to do.

It's OK to have the wrestle. It's OK to not want to do the cleaning or the service, or the work for your employer you're being paid to do. I don't recommend giving all that up. There are consequences if you decide not to do certain things and you must understand that.

But what I truly want you to understand is that, if you can change your thought process—if you can do things because you want to do them (even if they're terrible, horrible, unpleasant tasks)—you become the master of your fate. You are once again the director of your life.

Deliberately deciding how you think about things can make a profound difference. You can do the dishes with a grumbling attitude and get the reward of a grumbling heart, or you can do the dishes because you want to make your wife or your father happy—and, in turn, become happy yourself.

You're getting the dishes done either way, but choosing to do them with a positive attitude gives you immediate personal satisfaction.

Choose your thoughts. Direct your life. Upskill your happiness. But do it because you want to.

Remember there are no obligations. It's up to you. Reflect. Ponder. Appreciate. Value. Focus. Decide. 'Cause for you to be motivated correctly yagottawanna.

– ACTIVITY –

Take a look at this week's calendar. Which activities immediately jump to mind as ones that you were thinking were I have to events? Now take a pen and paper and write down three good things that will come as a result of your participation. Think deep. What relationships can be strengthened? What can you learn or overcome? There. You're once again in charge of your life.

Reclaim your power to choose and recognize the choice in every activity.

"The purpose of life is to discover your gift.
The work of life is to develop it.
The meaning of life is to give your gift away."
— *David Viscott*

CHAPTER 8

SKILL #3 – LIFT SOMEONE ELSE

CONGRATULATIONS. YOU'RE NOW INTO SKILL #3, which is all about connecting ourselves to others through service. Deliberate, premeditated compassion. You will likely be surprised by some of the research in this skill.

Now, as I'm sure you are recognizing, there are multiple ways you can approach each skill. And each skill contains many sub-skills. You obviously don't have to master *all* of them to be happier. In fact, I bet you're recognizing things in your life right now where this training has brought things to your mind that show you have a good life. You've been able to focus on what's going right in your life, and you may have already been surprised at how many awesome blessings you currently have.

So while you don't need to master *all* of the skills, isn't it incredible to think of the many different ways we can sharpen and improve our mental focus? How we can deliberately do things to enjoy deeper personal relationships? How we can SAVOR THE NOW and be fully present? And how we can intentionally increase our gratitude levels and almost immediately feel the swellings of positive energy in our lives? Now, think how those are just the first *two* skills. Imagine how empowered you're going to be when you finish this whole book.

Here are some interesting statistics. We're going to talk about some practices in this module that seem dead obvious. It'll seem like total no-brainer stuff, yet common sense is not always common practice.

So here are some startling numbers. The National Center for Health Statistics reported on the rising use of antidepressants.

The Center figures that about one in every 10 Americans takes an antidepressant, which is the third most common prescription medication taken by Americans in 2005-2008 (which is the latest period in which prescription drug use data was collected).

Some of the stand-out numbers from their report[13]:
- 23% of women in their 40s and 50s take antidepressants—the highest of any group identified by age or sex (that's nearly ONE out of every FOUR women for that age group).
- Women are 2.5 times more likely to be taking antidepressants than men.
- Less than a third of Americans who are taking a single antidepressant have seen a mental health professional in the past year.
- Antidepressant use does not vary by income status.

The most astounding numbers show that antidepressant use in America for teens and adults has increased by almost 400% since 1994.

Other interesting numbers:
- Forbes reports 52% of Americans are unhappy at work[14]
- Gallup reports 70% of U.S. workers are not engaged at work
- A 2011 Harris Poll[15] reports that only 33% of Americans consider themselves "very happy"

I point these statistics out because there's something we can do about it.

This is why you're going to love Core Happiness Skill #3: LIFT SOMEONE ELSE.

This is the service component to the Core Skills of Happiness. There's some scientific research out there that says when people strive to be happier it can actually backfire and lessen their overall life satisfaction levels. However, the research further indicates this can commonly happen when people strive to be happy on their own. In other words, they miss the required social aspect of happiness—we are social creatures. We need others and we need strong social connections.

HELP ANOTHER AND YOU'LL HELP YOURSELF

This concept will come as no surprise to anyone—we feel joy when we lift and serve others.

For centuries, well-known poets, philosophers, and sharp-witted social, moral, and religious leaders have reiterated the idea that kindness generates happiness. Of course we know it, duh, but it doesn't mean we practice it. We get so caught up in the frenzy of satisfying our own wants and needs that we soon feel starved or empty; like we have nothing left to give—and that if we were to give we would then be left completely dry.

But it's self-deception. The quickest, easiest way out of this toxic mental sinkhole is to reach down and LIFT SOMEONE ELSE up.

Here's some research on the benefits of serving.

According to the 2010 UnitedHealthcare Do Good. Live Well. Survey[16], 68% of those who volunteered said it made them physically healthier. Volunteers rated higher in physical strength and stamina as well as immunity and overall energy levels.

Volunteers also reported it has increased their emotional well-being and their ability to socialize, and deepened their sense of purpose in life. 96% of the volunteers surveyed said it made them happier, 95% said it improved their emotional health, and 94% said it boosted their self-esteem.

The positive effects were even more pronounced for those who volunteer on a regular basis.

Possibly the most surprising detail emerging from the research is that, despite the many benefits of service, a whopping 59% of those surveyed had not participated in any volunteer activities in the past year. Looks like we have lots of opportunities to increase our happiness levels.

Question for you: How are you doing with service? What groups do you volunteer for? How regularly do you volunteer? And how do you feel when you serve?

The research indicates we can dramatically improve our happiness levels when we engage in sincere, meaningful service. Now, if you are or have participated in service and didn't feel any boost … in fact, maybe you felt annoyed or put out … I want to remind you about the Yougottawanna principle from the last chapter. Strive to bring your motivations internal. Serve because you *want to*, not out of guilt or obligation. Make it your willing choice and you will find deeper satisfaction and increased love.

Here's some more research. Researchers in England[17] conducted an experiment where they randomly assigned participants to one of three groups. The first group was instructed to perform an act of kindness daily for ten days. The second was instructed to do something new for each of those ten days. The third was the control group receiving no instruction.

Before and after the experiment, participants were given a survey measuring their life satisfaction. After the ten days, both those who practiced acts of kindness and those who engaged in novel acts expressed a significant boost in their happiness levels, while the third group didn't get any happier.

The findings suggest not only can we deliberately improve our life satisfaction by engaging in random acts of kindness but, more importantly, we can feel the benefits in as little as ten days.

And for the last little bit of scientific research for you to digest today, social scientists Christian Smith and Hilary Davidson, from the University of Notre Dame, surveyed 2,000 individuals over a five-year period.[18] They found that Americans who consider themselves "very happy" volunteer an average of 5.8 hours per month. Those who considered themselves "unhappy" only volunteered .6 hours.

They put their findings in a book, *The Paradox of Generosity*. Not only did they find a correlation between giving and happiness but they also identified causation—in other words, giving *causes* happiness. Christian Smith says, "We don't argue it's one-way. We argue it's circular. The more happy and healthy and directed one is in life, the more generous one is likely to be, although that's not guaranteed. It works as an upward spiral where everything works together, or it works sometimes as a downward spiral if people aren't generous."

Note: In their testing, they found that having a generous mentality had to be sustained over time. One-time experiments of generosity did very little to elevate a person's happiness levels over time.

— ACTIVITY —

OK. This is going to be fun. Today, I want you to practice a random act of kindness. You pick what you do, just make sure this is pre-meditated. When you're done, write about it in your journal.

PREMEDITATED COMPASSION

Increasing compassion is one of the core skills of happiness. Matthieu Ricard is regarded as the happiest man alive. He was given that title because there is a way to measure happiness in the brain. You do that by measuring the activation levels of the left prefrontal cortex vs. the right prefrontal cortex. When they measured him, his results were off the charts. He was by far the happiest man ever measured by science. After the test he was asked what he was thinking about. He said he was meditating on compassion.

Compassion literally means "to suffer together". *Wait? What? Suffering is tied to happiness?*

Compassion is different from empathy, though closely linked. With empathy we *feel* something for someone else. Through compassion we *act* on those feelings.

According to the Greater Good Science Center at UC Berkley[19], when we feel compassion our heart rate slows down and we secrete oxytocin, activating the pleasure circuits in the brain. They go on to say compassionate people are more optimistic, make better spouses, are more supportive to friends, are less vindictive, and report feeling more positive emotions like joy and contentment. They're also more resistant to stress and anxiety.

Deliberately practice compassion by recognizing other people's suffering and intentionally acting so as to relieve that pain.

Now, if you want to get the full benefits from serving, make sure you're giving something up that's important to you—whether that's time, money or conveniences. And make sure it's for someone else. Don't get caught in the trap of serving others with the secret hope they will serve you back. The point is to get our focus off of ourselves and onto someone else. We need to learn to deeply care about someone else, care more about them than whatever it is we are sacrificing.

Our "me mindset" is what got us into these problems in the first place. Sometimes we need to take drastic steps to change from our constantly thinking about ourselves mindset to where we deliberately take time to pay attention to others.

To enjoy stronger feelings of peace, contentment, purpose, and meaning we need to reconnect with the family of man. Purposefully serving is an awesome way to do this.

I hope you've been regularly and actively participating in the activities contained in the Feed Your Happy app. This app is the mobile component of this book. It's your Mobile Mindset Conditioning app. Make sure you set the reminders in the app so they can help you mentally condition yourself into a positive mental lifestyle … and do this when you're out and about living.

– ACTIVITY –

Today's activity comes straight from the Feed Your Happy app. It's my favorite activity in the app. Today, I want you to give a chocolate bar away to someone. Now, before you go and do this I want to explain where you will see the benefits. See this is all about pre-meditated compassion.

Unless you have a chocolate bar already lying around on your desk or something—and, who knows, maybe you do— unless you've already got the chocolate bar, you're going to be thinking about how you're going to complete this activity while you're going to the store to purchase the candy bar. You're going to be imaging up scenes where you give the bar to someone. Maybe you haven't quite figured out yet whom you're going to give it to. As you play these scenes out in your head you will feel the excitement of anticipation.

Then, when you actually give the chocolate bar away, you're going to feel that burst of energy again. The energy you felt with the anticipation will come back even stronger as you act on your kind intentions.

And lastly, when you then come back and write about it, you'll relive those feelings for the third time. Breakfast, lunch, and dinner, baby. That's what Feeding Your Happy is all about.

RESEARCH ON GENEROSITY

Let's talk about a different aspect of serving—the kind of serving we do when we practice generosity.

First off, I've got to tell you I love generous people. Charitable people. I've done a ton of film work where I've met and interviewed some of the most generous and also wealthiest people around. The people I've met who generously give of their time, talents, or treasures are some of the happiest people on Earth. And they make me want to be more like them.

Wealth is funny stuff. How is it that some say, "Money is the root of all evil" and they can point out how money, or the love of money, has destroyed individuals and families? The fighting over money causes divorce and lawsuits, bitterness, anger, and resentment while, on the complete other spectrum of life, some people can enjoy enormous wealth and yet they're the kindest, most generous people you will ever meet? They're philanthropists. They use their means to generously bless others.

It's not the money—it's the generosity that makes the difference. It's their mindset.

For these people, these generous people, money doesn't canker them. It doesn't spoil them. In fact, it seems to breathe life into them. In the next section, I'll tell you a story about one generous man I filmed once who completely changed my perspective on wealth.

Generosity is the key. Giving sparks happiness, which, in turn, triggers more giving and more happiness.

A joint study[20] by researchers at the Harvard Business School and social scientists at the University of British Columbia established an upward spiral connection between giving and happiness. Participants were asked to reflect on a time when they spent a certain sum of money on themselves or someone else.

Those who thought about making a purchase for someone else reported feeling significantly happier while reminiscing, plus they were more likely to choose to spend a windfall on someone else in the near future.

Researchers concluded, "These data offer one potential path to sustainable happiness: prosocial spending increases happiness which in turn encourages prosocial spending."

I like that: *sustainable happiness.*

Let's look deeper into the benefits of giving.

Generosity creates a positive paradox—when we give we also receive. Numerous studies have confirmed that generous givers enjoy longer, happier, healthier lives.

One study[21] conduced in 1999 by Doug Oman of the University of California, Berkley found that "elderly people who volunteered for two or more organizations were 44 percent less likely to die over a five-year period than were non-volunteers." 44% less likely to die?

Dr. Stephen Post has written an entire book on the subject. In *Why Good Things Happen to Good People* Post cites clinical data that outlines the physical, mental, and social health benefits that come from a life of giving. Even people with chronic illnesses like HIV, multiple sclerosis, and heart conditions have been shown to experience health benefits by increasing their giving habits.

– ACTIVITY –

Today, practice increasing your generosity. Give anonymously. Send a friend cash. Donate to a cause. Give to a stranger in need. You decide how much. Feel the benefits of being a philanthropist.

Don't forget to use your journal to write about it.

AN ABUNDANCE MENTALITY

As a filmmaker, I'm fortunate to be able to meet and interview some amazing people. I remember one man in particular. I was doing a short film on him because all of his donations to a particular university had totaled over fifty million dollars. And he wasn't done.

I had an idea to create a film about him where he told what he believed. One of the things I was surprised to hear him say was, "I believe the more I give the more capacity I have to give again."

It surprised me. I had grown up with a scarcity mentality. I thought that when you gave things away they were gone. According to this man, when you give you are blessed with an abundance to give more. But it's not just him. He was the first man of extreme wealth that I interviewed personally but he was not the last, nor was he alone in his abundance mentality. In fact, most every wealthy person I've ever filmed who had a philanthropic heart reiterated the same idea.

"The more I give the more capacity I have to give again."

It took me years to trust this. To try this. To abandon the scarcity mentality for one of abundance.

I know a man who overcame a life of scarcity thinking. He felt he was poor and that he would forever be poor. He was constantly focusing on what he felt was his lack in life. This negative thinking beat him down and his obsession with his feelings of scarcity became self-fulfilling prophecies.

Then he had a transformation.

He decided he was going to deliberately choose a mind of abundance. He decided he was going to turn his finances over to God. He said, "If God says he notices a sparrow that falls from a tree … and that He clothes the lilies of the field … surely He can help me with my finances. I'm going to turn my financial worries over to Him and have faith." My friend realized that in doing this he would need to keep his faith up, so he found a mental trigger that would help him repeatedly put himself into this faith mindset, this abundance mindset. He said when he sees a coin on the ground it reminds him, "Oh, yeah. God is my provider and, look, He's got such an abundance it's even spilling out into the street."

That's an awesome mental trigger, a great way to deliberately get yourself into a mindset of abundance.

The abundant mindset is the mindset of success. It's the optimist's mindset. It's an open-ended approach to life.

Think about it, will we ever run out of creativity? If we share ideas or love or kindness, do we feel empty? No. The opposite. The more love we give away the more love we have to give.

This is the abundance mindset. It is the way we grow to become more. To live a life of purpose and meaning.

If you want to be happy—today—find a way to give. It can be money, time, or your talents. It may be something you've squandered. Maybe you feel so pressed for time, all the time, every day. You selfishly hold tight to any free time like a man clutching a hand full of sand with his fist. Picture this: He's got a fist full of sand but the tighter he grips it the more the sand slips out between his fingers and is lost.

Change your mindset. Give. Open your hand full of sand. You'll notice the sand stays in place and can be freely shared. As you give, you will find your focus changes. For example, anyone who has time to volunteer with a youth group obviously has time to spare. Once you start to practice it you will also start to feel it. You will begin to live a life of abundance.

– ACTIVITY –

Practice abundance. Many people who transition from a scarcity mentality to a mindset of abundance express the dramatic change that comes into their lives—especially in terms of their happiness levels.

Have you ever withheld a compliment worrying it would upset the balance of power? Or obsessed over your paycheck because you didn't have "enough"? That's the scarcity sinkhole. Switch your mindset. Start to share. Give your time, your knowledge, your experience. Share compliments and credit. Donate money to a friend or a cause. Contribute any way and every way you can. It's hard to feel as though your resources are limited or scarce when you're giving them away. Do it today.

Begin by writing down three things you have an abundance of that you can give to help others likewise prosper.

JOURNEY TO THE MEANINGFUL LIFE

As we take you through the Seven Core Skills of Everyday Happiness I want to point out the end goal. It's important to know where you're headed, right?

First off, you're going to learn to have joy in the journey, so don't be confused thinking that the end goal is happiness. That's the old mindset. Happiness should be enjoyed every day all along the way. It's part of the process. In fact, if we focus so much on getting to the destination (for example if we were to focus so much on college graduation) we might find the destination is empty. The reward *is* the journey, the education and personal growth we experience each day of our life.

Still, the destination is important. Our end goal is to help you in your journey to a meaningful life. To have purpose. To live abundantly.

You will begin enjoying this life long before you get near it as a destination, but it's important to be focused on where you're heading.

Eleanor Roosevelt said, "The purpose of life, after all, is to live it, to taste experience to the utmost, to reach out eagerly and without fear for newer and richer experience."

Oscar Wilde said, "To live is the rarest thing in the world. Most people exist, that is all."

As we head along this journey, be aware of the kind of life you would like to live. To create. To savor. This is not a one-size-fits-all result. Your life of purpose and meaning will be completely different from mine or that of the person sitting next to you. Be prepared to start searching within yourself to find what talents and abilities you've been given that you will want to use to their fullest.

Then go 'till the whistle blows.

Because this is so important, I will remind you of the quote I shared earlier by David Viscott:

"The purpose of life is to discover your gift.
   The work of life is to develop it.
   The meaning of life is to give your gift away."

This idea is the central foundation to this mindset training book. If you soak in this one lesson, if you find your calling, your mission, your purpose, if you find what contribution *only you* can provide, imagine the self-confidence you will receive each day that you're working for and striving for attaining your ultimate gift. Imagine the satisfaction that comes from having a life filled with purpose and meaning.

FIND YOUR CALLING

We all want to belong to something larger. To feel like our lives count. That we matter. Many scholars cite that finding our "calling" or purpose or passion in life is the key. Discover what feels rewarding to you and go after it. Find a problem to solve. Blend your talents to alleviate social ills. Develop your inner voice and set it free.

Don't confuse having a job with having a purpose. If you feel you're coasting, change your course and do something challenging. Seize your gifts. These are just a few ideas to get you thinking. Ultimately, you must decide what your passion is—what your life's work, or your contribution will be.

There's only *one person* in all the seven billion people on this planet who has your particular set of skills, talents, and experiences. To quote counsel given to Esther from the Bible, "And who knows but that you have come to your royal position for such a time as this?" (Esther 4:14)

Your life has a purpose and meaning. It's up to you to discover what that is.

I love this quote by Mark Twain: "The two most important days in your life are: the day you are born, and the day you find out why."

Wise words, right?

In his book, *Man's Search for Meaning*, Viktor Frankl wrote about those who survived the horrors of the Nazi concentration camps. Many could not handle the inhumane treatment and chose suicide. They would run into the electric barbed wire fences or find other ways to end it quickly. Others simply gave up.

He talked about how there were signs when a person was giving up and how they could tell how many days they would last before their hearts would give out. But then there were the survivors. Victor Frankl quoted Friedrich Nietzsche (a German philosopher) who said, "Those who have a 'why' to live can bear with almost any 'how'."

He talked about those who found the will to live for another human being who might be waiting for him or those who became conscious of an unfinished work that *only they* could produce.

After his horrible experiences in the concentration camps he served as a psychiatrist helping many people. Suicide continued to be a problem, but surprisingly many of the people prone to suicide were not those who were being tortured by terrible circumstances but those who had ample "success" and leisure. He said, "Life is never made unbearable by circumstances, but only by lack of meaning and purpose."

Viktor Frankl counseled, "One should not search for an abstract meaning of life. Everyone has his own specific vocation or mission in life to carry out a concrete assignment which demands fulfillment. Therein he cannot be replaced, nor can his life be repeated. Thus, everyone's task is as unique as is his specific opportunity to implement it."

That's deep. *Everyone has his or her own mission in life to carry out... Their own contribution to make...*

Brendon Burchard, a popular motivational speaker, is famous for pointing out that at the end of our lives we will look back and ask three questions: Did we live? Did we love? Did we matter?

They're good questions to ask, a good barometric reading on how we're doing in living a happy, fulfilling life.

So how do we do it? How do we find out what our calling is? What our purpose is? May I suggest it starts by living intentionally?

There are principles I've learned as a commercial film director that you can apply in your life, which will bring you amazing purpose and happiness.

Here's the foundational principle: filmmakers don't take pictures—they make them. There's a huge difference. They start with a script. A plan. They visualize it. They even hire an artist to storyboard each scene.

Before each day of filming they compose a shot list—a list detailing out every shot they hope to take. They envision the day. They visualize exactly how they hope the day will go. They see each and every scene before they create it. In their minds they can see where the sun will be at any particular point in the day for the corresponding scene. They expect it and anticipate it. If the light isn't going to be what they want naturally, they create it. They set up lights to capture exactly the mood or feeling they want to achieve.

The point is filmmaking is completely, 100% pre-meditated. It's orchestrated. Designed. And carried out.

You can do this with your life. Learn to live with intention. Don't just take what the day brings you. Don't wing it or fake it. And don't let other people or circumstances dictate how your day is gong to turn out. It's up to you. Envision it. Craft it. Create it.

Understand that social connections matter. Participate in meaningful service deliberately. Consciously. Go out of your way to help others.

Be the creator of your life. Direct it. Learn to live with intention—as you do you can focus on the bigger picture. *Your* bigger picture. What contribution are you going to make?

In the movie *Dead Poets Society* Robin Williams played the lovable John Keating, a professor who used unorthodox teaching methods to get his message through. In one stirring scene where he reminds the students their time on Earth is precious and short, he quotes the poem, *Oh Me! Oh Life!* by Walt Whitman, where he questions the meaning and purpose of his life.

The character John Keating cries out, "We don't read and write poetry because it's cute… We read and write poetry because we are members of the human race… And the human race is filled with passion… And medicine, law, business, engineering, these are noble pursuits and necessary to sustain life… But poetry, beauty, romance, love … *these* are what we stay alive for." With wrapped attention Keating almost whispers these last words… "What good amid these, oh me, oh life? Answer. That you are here … that life exists, and identity; that the powerful play goes on and you may contribute a verse. That the powerful play goes on and you may contribute a verse… What will your verse be?"

Now I ask you… Have you figured it out yet? Have you found your calling?

"What will YOUR verse be?"

— ACTIVITY —

This activity is the heart of this whole mindset training. I suggest you repeat this activity several times as you hone in on what your calling is in life, what your purpose is here. If you discover this for yourself and then have the courage to follow and fulfill it, you will have a life of purpose and meaning and happiness will flow through you.

Right now, spend a few minutes thinking about what you think your mission or your calling in life is. What will your verse be? What contribution do you hope to make? Spend time thinking about it then write it down. This will give you the larger vision purpose to where you can then direct all the rest of your energies.

"May your choices reflect your hopes, not your fears."
— *Nelson Mandela*

CHAPTER 9
SKILL #4 – DON'T WORRY

CONGRATULATIONS ON MAKING IT TO SKILL #4. You're doing a wonderful job. Not just for you, but for those around you. You're aware of how contagious positive or negative attitudes can be. You're conditioning your mind to be an optimist and to enjoy all the zest for life that you get with an optimistic lifestyle.

I want to pause for a moment before we jump into this new section to share the story of a friend. This young man—well, he was a young man when he started out on this downward path—was eighteen years old when he started experimenting with drugs. He used them as an escape from life, but it turns out they didn't help him escape at all. They basically put him to sleep.

He spent nearly a decade of his life in the darkest of places. He was on the run from the law. He was in and out of various relationships, never with any lasting satisfaction. He had no ambition or drive. He would sit around in his apartment with his buddies doing drugs and wishing his life away.

Then he finally "came to himself". Just recently he's bounced out of this self-destructive lifestyle. He's gaining hope and vigor in life again, and he's doing it by participating … by being active in the creation of his life. He's visualized out what he wants his life to be like and he's striving daily to bring that about.

I share this story not as a warning of the destructive nature of drugs, though that is so true. Rather, I share this story as an example of what happens when someone wakes up. When they once more become conscious, they become more aware of their circumstances. I'm sure you can picture in your mind the difference this young man is experiencing in his life as he's now filled with hope and enthusiasm for his future. His mind is his once more. His *life* is his once more. He's in control of his circumstances and he's directing his future.

In many ways, we are often like this young man. We get lulled to sleep; conditioned by society to just "go with the flow". We live out of habit instead of intention. Life "just happens" and we "just let it". This kind of passive thinking is like a drug. It takes away our ability to feel things. Passive thinking dulls our thinking and numbs our joys.

It's not until we wake up, it's not until we become fully conscious of how our thoughts are either opening doors or closing doors before us that we break out of our stupor. The more we then take back control of our thoughts, and refuse to allow society or circumstance or setbacks to shape our thinking, the more we will wake up; the more we will become alive again and experience the full goodness of life.

That's what you're doing with this training. Remember the goal is to condition your mind to choosing the most successful mindset possible—the deliberate mindset.

GET RID OF STRESS, ANXIETY, AND WORRY

So welcome to Skill #4 – DON'T WORRY. This is one of my favorites because we'll share how you can effectively relieve stress and anxiety from your life.

You've done an amazing job so far. You've gone step-by-step through each of the Core Skills of Happiness. Again, we are following industry-standard best practices to bring this to you in the most effective manner possible. And that's truly what we want, right? We want this to be effective, to work, to make that seismic change in your life, in your relationships, your self-confidence, your clarity, and your sense of self-purpose. Keep going. You're going to love this chapter.

So we're now in the mental detox skill. Along with building a positive mental lifestyle—adding focus and clarity to our lives—sometimes there's some cleaning that needs to be done. Some disinfecting. This module will help you clean up that "Stinkin' Thinkin'" as Zig Ziglar would always say.

The skill of DON'T WORRY is such an important skill. It's what separates you from your environment. You know, where you can sometimes feel stuck or trapped or victimized by the circumstances around you.

As Mahatma Gandhi so eloquently stated, "Nothing wastes the body like worry." Worry is powerful, but negative, energy. It's creative and imaginative yet also destructive. It brings fear, stress, and anxiety. Worry comes from inventing stories inside our brains, stories with bad endings. Reverse the flow. Realize you can rewrite the endings to envision a positive outcome. This skill is about learning to remove mental toxins of stress, anxiety, and despondency from your life. By eliminating negative thoughts we make room for positives.

DON'T FEED YOUR FEARS

Let's start out talking about how not to feed our fears.

We all have them—those noisy little irrational fears that keep us still or silent or in a slump. They whisper their seductive can'ts into your ears—you're not good enough. Or smart enough. Or pretty enough. They lie. They stand between you and your dreams, your achievements or your relationships, often between you and your happiness.

They're hungry little beasts. But therein lies their weakness. In order for them to thrive they need you to believe in them—sometimes just enough to keep them around.

Why not cut off their power source? Stop trusting. Stop listening. Stop taking counsel from those lying little fears. Start believing in the possibilities of you.

So how do you do that? You start something. Something that stretches you. Something scary. Or hard. Or scary-hard.

Action cures fears. Inaction feeds them. Ever noticed how the longer you wait the louder and more convincing your fears become? That's because we're so focused on the terrible outcomes we've imagined up at the end of our story.

When we begin—when we start to move or take action—our thoughts are forced to change as well. They can't be fully focused on the end consequence because at least part of your brainpower is now devoted to what the next step or action is going to be.

Gregory Berns, author of, *Iconoclast: A Neuroscientist Reveals How to Think Differently*, writes about how to activate your brain more fully by introducing controlled friction. He says that our brain gains "new insights from people and new environments—any circumstance in which the brain has a hard time predicting what will come next."

Deliberately forcing your brain to process unpredictability will help keep your fear reeling backwards as it moves out of the way of your noble pursuits. Richie Norton, in his book, *The Power of Starting Something Stupid*, relates many stories behind people who learned the surprising secret to success—you start.

– ACTIVITY –

Here's what I want you to do for today's activity. Write down the reasons your boss, your spouse, your significant other, or your parents like you. This will help you clear up some of the mental baggage that may have been building up.

Write down the reasons in your journal.

HOW TO REWRITE STRESS

Let's talk about stress. Where does it come from? If you think about it, generally it comes from a bad story we've told ourselves. You know, we imagine up some horrible ending that might-could-maybe-possibly happen.

We work that imaginary story through our heads until the possibility becomes a probability. Our shoulders tense up. Our stomachs churn. It's awful. Especially since it can be avoided.

There's a pithy quote attributed to the great Mark Twain that says, "I've lived through some terrible things in my life—some of which actually happened."

How often do we imagine up terrible endings? We envision horrible misfortunes and stress and fret and worry until we start to focus on our next wretched possibility—and then we stress and fret and worry again. It's an awful cycle. And we don't even realize we're doing it.

We self-sabotage our own peace and happiness by the stories we tell ourselves in our heads.

It's time to stop the bad storytelling. When you start to feel stressed, take a moment to stop and think about what it is you're feeling stressed about. You may realize you've told yourself a story with a bad ending. This is your chance. Recognize that's an imaginary story. Then let's rewrite it.

Though we certainly wouldn't admit this to anyone, we do live in imaginary worlds as we conjure up dreadful possibilities that rarely ever materialize. So why not invent crazy-awesome outcomes? Why not use our imaginations to think up fanciful, positive endings to our stories—maybe even ludicrously impossible endings—that are good?

While it may seem irresponsible to think up such crazy stories, remember just moments before you were telling yourself stories that were working against you. As you tell yourself other possibilities, you are rewriting your outcomes. Sure, the crazy possibilities you've imagined up may never happen (just as the misfortunes may never happen), but one thing is for sure, you've written yourself in as the hero, the master over stress and anxiety.

There's a variation to this marred way of thinking: The Bad Fortuneteller. This is where the little voice inside your head starts predicting bad things happening to you. It forecasts misfortunes, reversals, bad luck, adversity, disasters, and tragic catastrophes.

I have to deal with this voice a ton when I fill the filmmaking role of a producer. A producer's job is to imagine up every possible thing that could go wrong—which piece of equipment might go down, which actor might not show, what to do if it rains or if a location falls through. Like lawyers looking for any possible loophole to plug, a producer must worry about all sorts of problems and plan for the worst. The problem with this mindset is that, in focusing on the worst possible outcomes, you also invite in that kind of negative energy. It's the Law of Attraction at its worst.

There is value in looking through negative possibilities and making plans to counter them, but the trick is you don't want to put undue focus on the negative. Although bad stuff is bound to happen, good stuff will likely happen too—especially if you're looking for the positives.

Here are a couple of strategies to countering The Bad Fortuneteller.

First, when a negative thought comes in predicting doom and destruction, think to yourself, *Well, that's* one *possibility,* and come up with another, less negative, outcome.

You may also brush the negative thought aside as you think, *How could you possibly know that?* This works for some people, but for others who have a highly developed sense of alarm, brushing warning voices aside will actually make the voices scream louder. They're warning voices after all. They want to make sure they're heard. For these people, I suggest strategy #2.

Here's Strategy #2 - I met a man who was an ex-Navy SEAL. He told me his plan for dealing with the stress and anxiety by playing the "what if" game. He would go through the mental exercise of envisioning the best and worst possible outcomes. As a thought would come into his head of possible tragedies, he would work it through his head. "Okay, if that were to happen…" and he would come up with a solution. He'd then flip the energy around and envision the best positive outcome and come up with a plan for how he would deal with that.

The point is that he was using his creative energy to come up with solutions. And even with his toughest problems he would have already visualized how he would deal with the issues, so stress was taken out of the equation.

Take active control of your imagination; don't let your imagination use you. It's a tool. Use it to your advantage.

You may want to read through this lesson several times as the strategies included in here are extremely effective for reducing stress and anxiety in our lives. Take time to pause and assess where your feeling of stress is originating… Recognize it's likely coming from a bad-ending story we're telling ourselves… Then go to work envisioning up better ending stories and manage and control your fears.

– ACTIVITY –

I want you to think of something that's stressing you out right now. Shouldn't be hard to come up with something, right? We all have things that bring stress, anxiety, or worry into our lives. Got it? Now I want you to consider what is causing that stress. Is it a horrible ending you've imagined? Do you have a bad fortuneteller predicting doom?

I want you to rewrite that story. In your journal, I want you to write an alternate ending. A crazy, seemingly impossible story. Maybe you have stormtroopers come into your story, or a heroic elf. It doesn't matter how crazy or irresponsible your storytelling is, what's important is that you decide what story you're telling yourself.

Write the new ending to your story in your journal and consider what this has done for your stress levels.

FAIL FAST. FAIL OFTEN

This axiom has become the mantra for innovation and entrepreneurship. What this means is that you take numerous small risks and quickly learn from them to discover what works and what doesn't. The process is used to validate a concept or assumption while it's in the paper stage rather than risk higher stakes after the idea involves engineering and production runs. With each mini-failure you pivot slightly as you search for a better path or combination of ideas. What they're really saying is learn fast, bounce back, and keep striving.

How can you apply this concept to your daily life? Life is, after all, experimental. Understanding that failures, mistakes, and missteps are part of the process may help you keep negative energy from discouraging you to strive again.

Learning to manage fear and anxiety in small, reasonable doses will help you avoid the stagnation that comes from fear avoidance or the debilitating effects of high levels of anxiety.

Did you hear that recurring theme again? *Actively manage your mindset.* Choose your mindset. Don't let it control you.

You'll want to avoid stagnation in your life. Often people get themselves into a rut of non-growth because they're afraid of failure. They've failed before and it didn't taste good. Plus, there are inherent risks. There are also *huge* risks by standing still, by not growing and developing.

We talked in an earlier lesson about one strategy for not feeding your fears—you start something scary. Here's a followup to that, a strategy that will help you continue to grow.

Time for a story.

I was a young director. I didn't have a ton of self-confidence in my abilities at this time. One thing I learned early that has made all the difference in my creative career was to surround myself with people who were waaaaay more talented than I was—then I'd allow them the freedom to make their contributions.

I remember working with an extremely talented editor named Krisi. She was phenomenal. She could take any idea, any concept I would bring in and she would bump it up several notches.

I'd work with her to get a cut to a scene or a film together. As she would get it to a point that resonated well, she'd say, "OK, let's try something new," and she'd start to re-cut this in a totally different way.

It terrified me.

She could sense my fear and anxiety and would remind me that we always had the other cut to go back to, "but let's audition this other idea."

I liked that idea, "Let's *audition* it." It means we're testing it out. We're getting a feel for it. There's no commitment here. Like an open casting call, we're looking for the best idea to step forward and thrill us.

What if you used this concept, this mental trigger in your life? What if you allowed yourself to do new, scary stuff? You allowed yourself to stretch and grow. You auditioned new roles and capabilities for yourself. If you find something doesn't work for you, that it doesn't resonate with you or that it just doesn't work out, remind yourself it was only an audition. Then actively audition the next idea.

Maybe the mantra should be *"Audition fast. Audition often."*

Try out new ideas. Give young, emerging ideas a shot. Allow yourself to have things not work out immediately, but learn and pivot and advance. You're the director of your life. Let's make your life truly award winning.

— ACTIVITY —

Move on. Think of a mistake you've made. Don't pretend it didn't happen or try to hide it (this just introduces guilt), instead accept it. Accept the mistake for what it was, and then move on. Today, I want you to write down a mistake you've made and allow yourself permission to move on.

Now remember, don't obsess on it. A good way not to spiral down with this activity (focusing on the ruts can sometimes put us in a rut) is to also write something good that came from the mistake—maybe a lesson you've learned or an expression of kindness someone else showed you. Write about your experience and move on.

AVOID COMPARISONS

To boost your happiness levels, master the skills of removing worry or negative energy from your life. Don't fret about what others may or may not think of you and resist the compulsion to compare yourself to others. Teddy Roosevelt said it best, "Comparison is the thief of joy." So true. Removing unnecessary anxieties is a challenging skill—one that must be practiced repeatedly to become natural and instinctive. But the better you get at it the happier you will feel.

You get that, right? Comparison robs you of your personal joy because your focus is outward—it's external. You're not centered in gratitude; in fact, you're *feeding* your ingratitude. You're focusing on things you feel you're lacking in life and obsessing over things you feel are out of your reach.

It's that "grass is always greener on the other side of the fence" idea. I had a wise friend named Paul educate me further on this once. He said, "The grass may be greener on the other side, and you're welcome to go there, but you can't take your mower and you can't take your fertilizer."

In other words, you can't expect to find yourself in any better situation if you're continuing to use your old, negative mindset. I've appreciated his wise counsel through the years.

So avoid comparisons. Be grateful for what you have. Center yourself in appreciating all the goodness that is currently yours. It's a powerful tool you can use to control and determine your happiness.

Now here's a counter idea. While you don't want to get caught in the trap of comparing yourself to others, you may want to use comparison as a skill, a tool to properly put situations in the right light.

What if you used comparisons to evaluate conditions in order to reveal options of good, better, or best?

For example, if I asked you how warm it is outside, and let's say it was 70°, is that hot or cold? Well, it entirely depends on what you're comparing it to. Maybe, if you're just coming out of a frigid winter and you hit your first 70° day, you'd likely say, "It's hot." If you've been in the middle of summer and the temperature drops from the high 90s to 70, you'd say, "It's cool."

The temperature—like most things in life—is purely relative. It is what it is. It's our perception that makes the difference.

So as this book is about empowering you with the tools and skills to deliberately choose the best, most productive mindset. Let's look at how we can use the skill of intentionally using comparisons to focus on what's going right in your life.

I have a friend who has been a clinical psychologist, but turned away from it when he learned about positive psychology. Now he teaches people how to empower their own lives through deliberate, conscious thought. His name is

Dr. Paul Jenkins and his practice is called "Live on Purpose".

He empowers people with conscious thought training where he teaches people to think about how they're thinking.

He takes a different approach where he actually teaches people to use comparison as a skill. He says we have two sides to our thinking. There's the evaluation mode where we compare present circumstances against past experiences. "Is right now better or worse?" Well, it depends entirely on what you're comparing present circumstances to.

He points out that in the evaluation mode things can always be better or worse. By realizing this, we can improve our assessment of things by being grateful that things are not as bad as they could be. There's that skill of gratitude popping up again.

On the flip side, he says we have a creative side too when we're thinking about how good things could be. The future thinking side of us is a creative side. Can things be better in our imaginations? Yes. They can also be worse, but again it comes down to what we're comparing things to.

Anxiety is a feeling that comes from anticipating future events that could be worse than we'd like them to be. Hope is the opposite. By teaching people to think about how they're thinking he empowers them with the ability to choose their mindsets.

You have the power to choose your mindset. And now you have one more tool with which to work.

— ACTIVITY —

Change your pass codes—not for protection, but for positivity. Think how often you log in each day. What if each time you entered your password you were encouraging your inner self with a hand-typed message? Change it to a pass phrase like: AimHi2day (aim high today), myKidzrgr8 (my kids are great), iknquitsm0kin (I can quit smoking), i4gveCheryl (I forgive Cheryl), or wrthw8n4 (worth waiting for).

This works especially well with a goal you're working on.
Think it. Believe it. Achieve it.

THE SCIENCE OF SMILING

What if you could look at someone's photograph and accurately predict how fortunate that person's life is going to turn out just by evaluating their smile? Actually you can.

In Harker and Keltner's famous "Yearbook Study[22]", researchers found that women who smiled the most lived happier lives, enjoyed more satisfying marriages, had fewer life setbacks, and expressed greater overall well-being.

The study, published in 2000, compared yearbook photos of 49 college-aged women with life outcome data collected over a 30-year period.

By observing the facial muscles—the zygomatic major (the muscle that turns the lip corners up) and the orbicularis oculi (the muscle surrounding the eyes)—researchers were able to identify authentic, genuine smiles, known in the scientific community as Duchenne (pronounced DoShen) smiles. They then coded the facial behaviors and compared them to long-term life outcomes. This revealed the connection between genuine smiles and overall well-being.

So if researchers can look at your smile, determine if it's truly sincere, and accurately predict how fortunate your life is going to turn out, does that also mean you can shape the fortunate outcomes of your life by fostering the kind of happiness that produces genuine smiles? Sounds like it's worth a shot. Give us a smile; we'll see you in thirty years.

Now here's something equally cool. You can use smiling as a skill too.

An effective happiness boost is to practice smiling. Smiling, we generally think, is a response or a reaction to something good. We think it comes *after*. But let's play the chicken or the egg paradox. What if the smile comes first?

Do this: Before you engage in a conversation with someone else, picture a friend you deeply love, an activity that brought you joy, or a funny moment that made you laugh. Relish in the memory long enough that you feel the corners of your mouth turning upward.

Smiling triggers activity in your brain that elicits other positive emotions and endorphins, allowing you to self-generate an upward spiral of happiness. You just have to start it.

But sometimes starting it can feel a bit daunting. You've heard the term, "Fake it 'till you make it?" That totally works with smiling.

While you can generally spot a fake smile when you see one, researchers say your brain can't tell if your own smile is fake or not.

An effective exercise is to hold a pen (or chopstick) sideways between your clenched teeth. This will force a smile that researchers have found releases the same endorphins and creates the same benefits you'd receive from an authentic smile including relieving stress, lowering blood pressure, and boosting immune systems.

So whether you're using the skills of remembering to spark a smile or a pen or a chopstick to force a smile, the start of a much brighter day begins with your conscious, deliberate decision to crack a smile first.

— ACTIVITY —

Do this for two whole minutes. I want you to take a pen or a chopstick and put it sideways in your mouth between your clenched teeth. You're forcing a smile. The research indicates your brain can't tell if this is a real or an imagined smile so it will start releasing endorphins. You will actually be triggering your brain to think you're happy.

There are multiple studies that show this works. My favorite study is the one where they had people do this while looking through Far Side comics and rating them on how funny they felt they were. That's the kind of science experiment I enjoy. It turns out the people who had a chopstick sideways in their mouth forcing a smile found the comics to be much funnier than those who did nothing special.

Imagine how much better life will be when we go through life smiling more than we currently do.

Ready? Do this for two minutes and write about your experiences.

ANGER IS A CHOICE

There's an old Cherokee parable known as "The Wolves Within". In it, a grandfather is teaching his grandson an important lesson.

"There's a fight that goes on inside each of us," says the elderly man. "It's a terrible fight between two wolves. One is evil. It is anger, envy, jealousy, sorrow, regret, greed and ego. The other is good. He is peace, joy, love, hope, serenity, compassion, kindness, and faith."

The grandson thought about this a moment. Then he asked, "Which wolf will win?"

The wise Cherokee replied, "The one you feed."

Just as you've learned happiness is a skill and a choice, so is anger. Honestly, though, anger doesn't take much effort. It's more of a hard-wired reaction. Where anger does take effort is in *resisting* it. Throughout the course of this training you've learned mindfulness techniques to actively employ in order to choose your mindset. You can do the same thing to resist anger.

For example, one storytelling exercise my wife and I engage in while we're driving is to come up with a crazy story to explain dangerous or erratic behavior from other motorists. A little white Mazda might cut us off and zoom dangerously down a canyon road at excessive speeds and my wife will tell me how his wife is probably going into labor and it's their first child. Or maybe he is trying to make it to the hospital so they can re-attach his left arm. We often make the stories wild and crazy, which makes us laugh. When we rewrite the stories, we allow ourselves to choose how we feel about their behavior.

It's much harder to get mad at a guy who's just trying to get his left arm re-attached. Focusing on his poor behavior isn't going to change the situation;

it's just going to foster negativity inside. Allowing yourself to get angry ruins your happiness not his or hers or theirs.

We want you to be happy, so we'll focus on best practices to keep you in the proper mindset.

Lou Holtz said, "Life is ten percent what happens to you and ninety percent how you respond to it."

TIME TO CALL THE WAAAAMBULANCE

Now let's talk about whining. No one would argue whining reveals a negative attitude. The very nature of the activity attracts and fuels pessimistic emotions. Complaining about a problem won't make it go away, but it sure can aggravate the situation. Once more I remind you that Jeffrey R. Holland wisely counseled, "No misfortune is so bad that whining about it won't make it worse." I love that quote especially since I'm a "recovering grump-a-holic".

Stop griping, grumbling, and bemoaning. Start by removing the negatives we say out loud. Don't say it and eventually you won't think it. If something is bothering you, fix it. If you can't fix it, change how you feel about it. Put yourself in someone else's shoes. Apply gratitude skills to find the good even in the unpleasant. Look for a lesson. Remember, there are so many positive ways to channel your energy.

Now, grudges are something different. These are long-term beasts. Grudges are hideous mental toxins that hang around for years. Whether they started as real or perceived offenses, whether we're "completely innocent" or maybe not so completely—we let the incident fester in our minds, aggravating the condition exponentially for ourselves.

Let's say the offense originated from a physical confrontation. Maybe there was actual physical pain that lasted for two hours or two days. By allowing ourselves to hold grudges, we transfer the physical discomfort into mental aggravation that doesn't dissipate.

The actual wound may have healed itself years ago, but through the lasting power of grudges we continue to feel fresh pain because of the mental poison we persistently circulate in our systems. Choose to relieve yourself from the mental toxin of a grudge by learning to "let it go".

Anger is a choice, complaining reveals a negative focus and grudges produce long-term toxins. But the best news is happiness is a choice too. It's a skill. A mindset. And it's increasingly becoming part of your natural lifestyle. Keep up the conditioning. Remember to use the Feed Your Happy app as your Mobile Mindset Conditioning tool.

— ACTIVITY —

Today, we're going to identify and eradicate.

Want to get rid of the mental toxins in grudges? First identify the people for whom you are holding a grudge. Is there someone you avoid? Is there someone for whom you wish harm? Someone you can't wait to backbite, ridicule, or snub?

There. You've identified a grudge. Now initiate the healing process. Recognize that the hurt is over. Give yourself permission to SAVOR THE NOW and move away from dwelling on the past. Reflect on how you've reacted and how you've allowed negative feelings to fester. Now freely forgive the other person (it's not for them, it's for you). Remove any feelings of revenge or retaliation.

Once you clear away the venom, do what you can to restore or rebuild relationships. In your heart wish them well. Congratulations. You're on the road to recovery.

Write about your experience in your journal.

REMOVE NEGATIVE SELF-TALK

Now let's look at replacing your negatives. Do any of these words describe you: Avoidant, volatile, bitter, begrudging, arrogant, self-absorbed, manipulative, irritated, timid, or angry?

They may signal opportunities for improvement—possibilities for greater happiness. Turn your negatives into positives. Be: Inclusive, calm, thankful, forgiving, thoughtful, kind, willing, assertive, and happy. Start one character trait at a time. Find one negative trait you'd like to remove and focus on developing its positive counterpart.

I believe in "Fake it 'till you make it." Actually, I believe in "Fake it 'till you *become* it."

I've read too many books and seen too many studies and talked to too many people not to believe that something changes inside of us when we allow ourselves to become a character trait. People who fake being confident eventually overcome their shyness. People who fake being assertive eventually become assertive.

Make a list of the qualities you most want to become. You want to be brave? *Be brave.* You want to be happy? *Be happy.* You want be trustworthy? *Be trustworthy.* You don't need permission; you just need to do it. Allow yourself to do it.

An unknown author with a quick whit chimed, "You can't litter negativity everywhere and then wonder why you've got a trashy life."

We all hold internal conversations as we go about each day. Psychologists call this "self-talk". The negative things we tell ourselves can be so destructive. Doubtful, discouraging, belittling comments can easily slip into our subconscious as we conduct our own internal running commentary on our lives.

Take a listen to what you're saying. Is it the voice of a critic or a cynic? Are you a sports announcer constantly over-evaluating each imperfection or misstep? Turn it around. Fire the announcer. Employ a constructive inner-voice who will lift, inspire, and encourage you. Mimic the cheering motivation of an understanding parent, friend or coach who wants to instill confidence, boost self-esteem, and inspire greatness as you strive for something better.

As I've been studying positive psychology and the amazing things we can do by reprogramming our mindsets, I've been surprised at how prevalent negativity is in society. I'm surprised at how I've been conditioned by negativity or that I condition with negativity.

Here's an example. You go out in your back yard to throw a football with your son. You give him a high spiral throw that he has to run to catch. As he's nearing the ball you yell, "Don't drop it!"

Now, what is that going to do to him? Think of the visuals that have to run through his head. He has to see himself *almost* catching the ball then *not* not-catching it. "Don't drop it!" Really?

What kind of straightforward and positive images would come into your head now if you were to say, "Hold it tight," or "You've got this one"?

Positive self-talk leads to positive outward expressions.

— ACTIVITY —

Enjoy National Day of No Whining today. That's the activity. Whatever today is, celebrate it like it's National Day of No Whining. Catch yourself if you start to complain and get off that negative thinking train. When you do catch yourself, spend a minute and find something to be grateful for. Use the skills you've learned so far to turn a negative into a positive.

Think of this quote by Dr. Seuss: "Today I shall behave as if this is the day I will be remembered."

Write about your experiences in your journal.

EXPECT GOOD THINGS TO HAPPEN

Expect good things to happen. Expect something wonderful is just over the horizon.

Suzy Kassem said, "Doubt kills more dreams than failure ever will." She was right. Sometimes we don't even attempt something because we think we can see how it's going to turn out. We imagine up negative possibilities ("probabilities" we tell ourselves) of how our stories will end. Maybe past "experience" has conditioned us into a state of learned helplessness where we think nothing we can do will change the outcome.

To counter this mentality, hockey Hall of Famer Wayne Gretzky provides this wisdom: "You miss 100% of the shots you don't take." So why not take some shots? Why not replace negative thoughts, agonizing over possible consequences, with hopeful ones unlocking potential? Do this: Imagine the positive possibilities. Follow Tom Hopkins' advice, "You begin by always expecting good things to happen."

Let's talk about the power of faith. Not church faith. Not faith unto salvation. There's tremendous power in that kind of faith, but I'll let you find your own path there. No, I want to talk about the power of believing good things are coming your way.

There's amazing power in this kind of faith. Some call it self-fulfilling prophecies. Some classify it under "expectancy theory". Others may call it the Law of Attraction. The fact remains; believing good things will happen brings about good things.

Gentlemen of the jury, I submit for evidence the power of the placebo effect.

You know about the placebo effect, right? Doctors will conduct a test where they administer real medicine to people, fake medicine to others (this is the placebo), and they'll have a control group who gets nothing and nothing changes.

Researchers used to think of the placebo effect as a "statistical annoyance". It got in the way of accurately evaluating legitimate medical therapies.

And it was always messing things up.

Depending on how convincingly the placebo was given, it would bring a cure rate of between 15 and 72%. Placebos with higher cure rates were administered more persuasively—two pills instead of one, injections work better than pills, repeated medical visits work better than a single treatment.

The fact is, placebos work. And they work because we believe in them.

Now, this isn't self-deception. It's not faking it or pretending. It's purely a product of expectation.

The cool thing is you can use the power of expectation in your life. You can use it as a skill to bring about good things.

Let's start with expecting good things will happen to you. Don't hope for it. Expect it.

How do you do this? Keep a gratitude journal every day. Set a regular time each day to write down three fortunate things that happen. After you do this for several weeks, you will be conditioned to look for good things to happen. You will begin to expect it. To believe it.

That's when you begin to use the power of faith to bring about good things in your life.

Good things are coming.

I hope you're using the digital gratitude journal in your Feed Your Happy app. Use the included reminder system to make this a regular mental conditioning exercise. I like the prompt, "Here are three fortunate things that happened today." And I like to write that at night, just before I go to bed.

This trains your brain during the daytime to look for and expect good things to happen. Then at night it conditions you to appreciate and express gratitude for your blessings.

Now let's take this one step further.

I like to use the power of lists. I like to take highlights from my gratitude journal and keep a running list of some of the most fortunate things to happen to me. These are events where I feel God has deliberately gotten involved in my life, where He leaves His fingerprints in the form of incredible luck and amazing coincidences. (I don't believe in coincidences—they're God's way of staying anonymous.)

Each entry is less than a sentence. I keep this on my phone where I can easily and regularly remember extraordinary blessings in my life.

What begins to happen when I intentionally look back at what I feel are God-given blessings is that I begin to believe good things are yet to come. I mean it doesn't make sense for Him to bless me throughout my life then suddenly stop.

Remembering and reflecting are tools I then use to anticipate and expect good things yet to come.

I love the words to the song "Something's coming" from the Broadway hit, *West Side Story*. It says:

"Could it be?
Yes, it could
Something's coming
Something good
If I can wait

Something's coming
I don't know what it is
But it is
Going to be great…

I got a feeling there's a miracle due
Gotta come through
Coming to me."[23]

Now whether you believe in God or not, or believe in the power of the Universe, Nature, or whatever, as you begin to make lists of fortunate things that have happened to you, you will begin to see a pattern—a repeated pattern of good things that have come into your life.

Use that pattern to forecast and believe that something good is coming. And it's just over the horizon.

— ACTIVITY —

Today, I want you to believe good things are going to happen. Make a note and stick it in your pocket or do something to remind you throughout the day to look for and expect something good to come your way. Later, or tomorrow, I want you to take out your journal and write about what you experienced. What amazing things happened? How did it affect you to be on the lookout for fortunate experiences?

"Only a life lived for others is a life worthwhile."
— Albert Einstein

CHAPTER 10

SKILL #5 – FOSTER POSITIVE RELATIONSHIPS

ALL RIGHT. YOU MADE IT TO SKILL #5. You're doing awesome. I hope you've been noticing the changes this training has made to your life. You're starting to be more aware of your thinking. You're likely catching yourself from heading down negative roads, and you're noticing more and more the fortunate things that are going on in your life. Awesome. Isn't it amazing how much of a difference it makes when we choose to deliberately focus on the good things in life?

You've probably started catching the negativity of those around you. You spot when your friends or family members start complaining or expressing grudges. As an observer, you've likely noticed that as they're expressing these emotions, they're not particularly cheerful. You're extra fortunate as you've been receiving this training. You've been learning to decide what you want to focus on and you're feeling more alive and awake. You're more conscious of the thinking—positive or negative—we all do and how it affects us. You're feeling powerful.

Now you're into Skill Five. This is the skill that probably makes the biggest difference in your long-term happiness levels. This skill is how to FOSTER POSITIVE RELATIONSHIPS.

Think about how much this affects happiness.

Imagine being the richest person in your city. You can buy absolutely anything. Picture yourself buying the most enormous mansion on the most prestigious hill. It's a gorgeous place. You've got tall, tall ceilings. Huge open areas. And you've got these windows that look over everything. The view is absolutely stunning.

Imagine yourself having all of this ... and feeling alone. Totally alone. I'm not talking about having some time to yourself, I'm talking about that deep feeling of loneliness—that nobody cares about you—you're all alone.

Now consider this. Do you feel rich? Is this wealth? True wealth? No. Of course not. True wealth is something money can't buy, yet we're conditioned by society to believe that money means happiness.

You can have it all monetarily and still not have happiness. Being genuinely happy is true success.

I read an article about Markus Persson, the newly minted billionaire who had developed Minecraft and sold it for 2.5 billion dollars. 2.5 billion! He was living the high life. He became an instant celebrity; everyone wanted a piece of him. He bought a $70 million dollar mansion complete with a wall of candy and began hosting wild parties.

He was living the good life, right? He was hugely "successful", right?

His tweets,[24] however, revealed he was bored and deeply lonely. In one tweet he said, "The problem with getting everything is you run out of reasons to keep trying, and human interaction becomes impossible due to imbalance."

At a party with all these other celebrities, he posted another tweet: "Hanging out in Ibiza with a bunch of friends and partying with famous people, able to do whatever I want, and I've never felt more isolated."

You can't have true success ... you can't have a life of happiness and fulfillment without strong social connections. Friendships matter. Relationships are key.

THE SCIENCE OF FRIENDSHIP

There's science behind this too. Numerous studies have been done showing that satisfying relationships are essential for overall health and well-being. Those with strong social connections live longer, enjoy healthier lives, are less prone to stress and anxiety, suffer less from depression, are less likely to have high blood pressure, and feel richer.

The opposite is also true. Scientists have found isolation and prolonged feelings of loneliness increase health risks comparable to cigarette smoking, high blood pressure, and obesity.

Here's some more science.

According to Christine Carter, Ph.D., a sociologist and happiness expert at UC Berkeley's Greater Good Science Center,[25] happy people are more likely to get married, have more fulfilling marriages, and have more friends.

Carter says, "The best predictor of happiness (and often health) is the quantity and quality of a person's social ties." Those who have many friends are less likely to experience sadness, depression, loneliness, low self-esteem, or have eating or sleeping disorders. Dr. Carter recommends building strong social networks (villages) for your children so they can develop friendships with kids of all ages and trusted parents, teachers, and community members.

Social connections matter. Friends matter. Relationships are vital. Yet when we're struggling, when life is hard and dark, what do we do? We retreat. We hide. We close ourselves off from the outside world and isolate ourselves.

When faced with challenges or setbacks in life don't disengage from your social connections—that may be when you need the resilient benefits of friendship the most.

— ACTIVITY —

Let's take a look at your best friends—your most important relationships. We all amass hundreds of digital friends on Facebook and other social media sites, but who are your true friends? Who could you call in the middle of the night to come and help you out? Who has been there for you when nobody else was? Who knows the real you and still wants to be your friend? These are your most important relationships. These are the people who genuinely care about you. Make sure you recognize them and nurture these relationships to make them last.

After you've thought through this exercise, take a few minutes to not only write who they are, but how you know they care about you.

LIVE WITH NO REGRETS

There's an awesome book by Bronnie Ware called *The Top Five Regrets of the Dying*. She wrote this after years of working with terminally ill patients.

Those near the end of their lives often look back with surprising clarity and insight. The busyness of life melts away, and with their fading health, they're left with time for quiet contemplation. It's amazing how clear life becomes when you take time to quietly think about it.

Among the top five most common regrets, people lamented, "I wish I had stayed in touch with my friends." In their final days they often felt a yearning to reconnect with old friends and express their love and appreciation for them.

Learn from this. Do what you can now to strengthen your most meaningful relationships.

Interestingly enough, the fifth most common regret that emerged from bedridden reflection was, "I wish that I had let myself be happier." They discovered all too late that happiness is a choice. Fortunately, you're coming to understand this early.

Here's one tip you can do to FOSTER POSITIVE RELATIONSHIPS: When you're with someone be all there. It's a "Be fully present" skill, part of the SAVOR THE NOW skill set. One way you can do this is to not put your cellphone out on the table in case you get a call or a text. Or maybe you place it between you and another person.

Researchers from Baylor University said this could negatively impact our relationships.[26]

They conducted two separate surveys and found that 46 percent of respondents reported feeling phone snubbed by their romantic partner—this is where they felt the cell phone took precedence over their face-to-face conversation. Nearly 23 percent said it caused an issue in their relationship and more than 36 percent of participants reported feeling depressed at least some of the time.

That's a bad habit. Do you live out of habit?

We often become tools of our tools. Ralph Waldo Emerson said, "Things are in the saddle, and ride mankind."

For example, do you use technology or does technology use you? Ask yourself whether you are compulsively checking your e-mail or Facebook. Are you always tethered to your cell phone?

If you want more positive relationships, make sure those you're with know they are more important than tools or technologies or distractions.

– ACTIVITY –

Let's learn from Bronnie Ware's book on the Top Five Regrets of the Dying. Let's reconnect with those we care about early. Today, I want you to call an old high school friend. Let them know you've been thinking about them as you reconnect. There's no embarrassment to be felt by falling out of touch with each other when the reason for you two reconnecting today is that you've been thinking about them. Show them they matter. Give them a call and write about your experiences in your journal.

INVEST IN PEOPLE

Amy Grant said, "The more time you invest in a marriage, the more valuable it becomes." So true. What other relationships do you enjoy? What other ways can you invest? Can you give more time, trust, hope, patience, compassion, or undivided attention to a relationship?

Think about your priority list. Are people high among your priorities? If so, do they know about it? How can you show this better?

Let's look at what occupies most of your time. Are there time wasters you can eliminate to spend more quality time with others? Technologies or gadgets you can put away to interact with humans? Distractions you can eliminate to make together time, undivided? Sacrifices you can make to put friends and loved ones above mere objects or things?

Now examine your commitments. Do you do what you say you're going to do for others? Can they count on you no matter what?

Lastly, there are those unspoken words. What kind words or expressions of love have you been holding back?

Don't save 'em. Invest.

Zig Ziglar said, "Spend time with those you love. One of these days you will say either, 'I wish I had,' or 'I'm glad I did.'"

– ACTIVITY –

Today, thank your boss. Write a thank you note for your boss. Express appreciation for the job you hold and the many skills and talents you've gained. Indicate how he or she helps you in your role and express sincere gratitude. Don't do this with any ulterior motive—you're not trying to get something here, you're giving back. You're expressing true gratitude for the good things you're experiencing by being employed.

BE INQUISITIVE

They say if you ask the right questions, you'll discover how truly fascinating someone is.

At their root, many of the happiness skills are about actively recognizing and appreciating meaningful things. Take, for example, those people around you.

How much do you know about them? Are you willing to learn more? Think about your relationships with co-workers. Do you understand the important milestones that have brought them into your circle? What experiences do they have that you can learn from? What motivates them? What guidance do they have for you?

Strong, healthy relationships are about giving time and attention. Make it a goal to get to know people better. Ask questions that get others to think; questions that show genuine interest and curiosity.

Anthony Robbins said, "Do what you did in the beginning of a relationship and there won't be an end."

Along with developing the skill of being inquisitive, being genuinely interested in others, we add the skill of paying attention.

If your goal is to increase the value of any relationship, remember Theodore Roosevelt's advice: "No one cares how much you know, until they know how much you care." By showing sincere interest, you can improve any relationship.

But what about that reclusive co-worker, with his single word responses? Open-ended questions with room for description and introspection might help.

People may not always tell you how they feel, but they will often show you. Pay attention. Look for non-verbal clues, body language, and changes in tonality. Don't judge, just listen. Go a step further—be extraordinarily polite. Be gracious and kind. Show empathy and understanding. Express sincere interest. Attention is the currency of friendships.

Another way you can improve your relationships is to always add value.

They say, "How you make others feel about themselves says a lot about you." It rings true.

Maslow's hierarchy of needs shows we all want to feel safe, loved, valued, and that we belong. So how much of a happiness booster are you? Are you fulfilling others' needs? We can all improve; here are a few suggestions: Give undivided attention. Put distractions away when having conversations. Use the person's name while talking with them. Listen more than you talk. Ask questions to genuinely learn from them. Give sincere compliments. Hold confidences. Don't badmouth others. Be inclusive.

By increasing your value-add skills you can be an important part of improving the self-confidence of those around you.

– ACTIVITY –

Let's say today's National Day of Listening. On this day I want you to consciously listen more. Don't be thinking of your response while someone else is talking. Genuinely take time to listen and learn.

You'll want to take time to write about this activity.

BE A SAFE HAVEN

Critics are everywhere. Maybe you've even got a critical voice inside of you. We're trained to think that way. Like a lawyer, we're conditioned to look for problems, weaknesses, and loopholes, and point them out.

But a critic isn't a builder. A critic doesn't create, contribute, or produce. You can't do that through destructive energy.

If you're prone to criticize, turn it around. Train your brain—and your speech—to lift, build, shape, enhance, strengthen, encourage, and inspire. Make your home or your cubicle a safe place where others can come and feel valued and supported. Recognize the good. Cheer valiant efforts. Be a builder of people.

We've all known someone like this—a person who makes everybody feel like a somebody.

When you're around them, you find you stand a little taller, speak with more confidence and become the best possible version of yourself. People like that are amazing. They turn the energy in any room positive.

Well, why not *be* a person like that? Why not throw compliments around like confetti? Why not boost and build? Why not pay more attention? Care a little more? You have the ability to constantly focus on others in a way that brings out their best. Go ahead; mirror the best people you admire. We could all use more people just like you.

Mother Teresa said, "The biggest disease today is not leprosy or tuberculosis, but rather the feeling of being unwanted."

Be a safe haven—especially for your spouse.

Want to hear the best marriage advice I ever got? It was about removing that critical voice inside our head that often slips out in the form of criticism and negativity.

It was this: Never say anything about your spouse to others that you wouldn't say if they were standing right next to you.

Awesome advice, right?

When we were engaged, my then-fiancée and I heard that advice and committed to it. Never say anything about your spouse to others that you wouldn't say if they were standing right next to you. It has made *all* the difference.

What you say about others when they're not around actually says more about you. It communicates to those you're with if you can be trusted. It separates faithful friends from friends of convenience.

Make it a habit to only say things you'd say if the person was there in the room. Think of the trust you would build with your spouse if they knew you were always saying positive things about them when they weren't around. If there are corrections that need to be expressed in order to fix or avoid problems, shouldn't they be said in private in the company of the one who needs to hear it? If your goal is to help them improve rather than point out faults, there will be no need to vent or express displeasure in the presence of others. A quote from the Apocrypha sums this up well. "A faithful friend is a strong defense. And he that hath found . . . one hath found a treasure" (Ecclesiasticus 6:14).

Stephen Covey said this another way. He said, "Be loyal to those who are not present. In doing so you build the trust of those who are present."

– ACTIVITY –

Begin today to never let anything come out of your mouth that you wouldn't say if that person were standing right next to you. Before you speak, apply this gossip-free practice: Think, Is it kind? True? And is it necessary?

REMOVE CRITICAL WORDS

Are there words you use that are negative in nature, that limit us or others or that put down or devalue people? "Can't" is one. "Ashamed" or "pathetic" or "inept" could be others. "Try" presupposes failure and "but" negates any words stated before it.

Negative words and phrases can have a crippling effect on our minds or on others when expressed. They don't express gratitude or appreciation, nor do they build or improve anything or anyone. They're just bad words that lead to toxic thinking. Flush 'em. Make a list of the "bad words" you currently use that you'd like to eliminate and get those garbage words out of your system.

Negative words have tremendous power.

Neuroscience studies have been carried out[27] where people were put in an fMRI scanner that measures the impulses in the brain. Then they flashed the word "no" for less than a second and the participants suddenly started producing stress hormones and neurotransmitters. *Psychology Today* reports[28] that "Just seeing a list of negative words for a few seconds will make a highly anxious or depressed person feel worse, and the more you ruminate on them, the more you can actually damage key structures that regulate your memory, feelings, and emotions."

Think of the power of hostile language ... especially spoken in anger.

According[29] to Andrew Newberg, M.D. and Mark Robert Waldman, an adjunct professor from Loyola Marymount University in Los Angeles,

"A single word has the power to influence the expression of genes that regulate physical and emotional stress." They compiled their research in a book called, *Words Can Change Your Brain: 12 Conversation Strategies to Build Trust, Resolve Conflict, and Increase Intimacy.*

In the book they recommend "compassionate communication" as a way to strengthen relationships and reduce conflict and suggest reversing the flow of negativity by saying 3 positive comments for every negative one, which has proven to be a positive technique for improving relationships.

Choose your words wisely. Start today by reducing or eliminating the negative words from your vocabulary.

— ACTIVITY —

Here's an easy and fun activity. Today, write a positive note to a friend or a loved one and then leave it in a place where they will easily find it. That's fun, right?

In your journal you can either write what you're going to do or you can come back and write about your experience. Pre-meditated kindness is awesomely effective for sparking your happiness levels.

SAVE THE RELATIONSHIP

All relationships have problems. Life's journey is never a smooth road. Whether there's a cooling, indifference, or outright bitterness (this is especially true when you've got teenagers), do what you can to save the relationship.

Time, as they say, heals all wounds—if we are willing to give it time without compounding the problem through frustrations and demands.

Don't cut ties. Let go of past offences. Avoid criticism. Improve gratitude and appreciation. Increase patience. Start afresh—applying the same amount of energy as you did when your relationship was new.

Give your time, your attention, your financial resources. There are so many ways you can put forth efforts to save your relationships and if you are successful you will be rewarded with increased and sustained love.

Regina Brett said, "Time heals almost everything. Give time, time."

If you're struggling with a relationship, you may wish to go back to some of the earlier lessons such as, "Anger is a choice" from the DON'T WORRY skill or "Forgiving others" from the SAVOR THE NOW skill.

Forgiveness is such a key to maintaining positive relationships. I shared this quote with you before by Akshay Dubey, it deserves repeating: "Healing doesn't mean the damage never existed. It means the damage no longer controls our lives."

Lastly, this isn't a marriage counseling course and I'm not a marriage counselor. There are wonderful services out there for you—use them. Save your relationships whenever you can.

Also, I'm not saying you should stay in an abusive relationship. Please, if you're in an abusive relationship, get help. I'm saying *whenever you can* save the relationship.

We live in a world of disposable items. Something stops working then we just replace it. If something starts looking old or maybe there's some other shiny thing catching our attention, we jump from one thing to the next hoping to find happiness.

Remember the lessons on the Myths of Happiness where we mistakenly think we'll find happiness outside of ourselves or in "more" or "next"?

DO NOT allow your relationships to fall into the trap of "disposable things". Positive relationships—strong human connections, a feeling of loving others and being loved back—are vital to true success.

Dr. Wayne Dyer said, "See the light in others, and treat them as if that is all you see."

I hope this training is teaching you that you have the power; you have incredible power to change the world around you simply by choosing a positive mindset. May this deepen and intensify your relationships as well.

– ACTIVITY –

Repair a broken friendship. Think of someone you haven't talked to in a long time, someone you once enjoyed spending time with but who has become distant now for whatever reason. Give them a call and catch up.

Then don't forget to write about it.

"What lies behind us and what lies ahead of us are tiny matters compared to what lies within us."
— Henry David Thoreau

CHAPTER 11

SKILL #6 – IMPROVE DAILY

ALL RIGHT, YOU'RE REALLY COOKING NOW. You've made it to Skill #6. Before we jump into this skill, I'd like to do a bit of a refresher on where we're heading. Remember, this is all about mindset conditioning. We're helping you train your brain—reprogram your mindset really—so that you can enjoy true success. This is the kind of success money can't buy.

I remember interviewing a wealthy man one time. He talked about what we wanted to do for his children. He said, "I can buy my kids cars ... and houses ... and land... But there are things money can't buy like integrity, a strong work ethic, responsibility, self-discipline, and self-confidence."

I'm sure he could have added "happiness" to the list.

True success, as you know, is about flourishing inside.

You've been doing great going through this training. You've learned how you can't be grateful and unhappy at the same time, and you've engaged in activities to deliberately focus on increasing your gratitude levels. Think back to how you felt doing some of the exercises when you reconnected with friends or recognized the fortunate blessings you *already* have in your life.

You've learned the value of being in the moment; of enjoying and savoring every good bit of life. You've practiced removing distractions from your life and you've maybe found a few ways where you were rushing too quickly from one moment to the next to properly enjoy the present. Good stuff.

You've learned and practiced deliberate, intentional service to others—pre-meditated compassion as I like to call it. You've learned how to detox from negative emotions and negative energy, helping to rid yourself of stress, anxiety, and worry.

Remember how to rewrite the stories that have been stressing you out?

You just learned about what value it holds for you to FOSTER POSITIVE RELATIONSHIPS and now you're here, right here, right now, enjoying the opportunity to learn the skill to IMPROVE DAILY.

After you go through this skill, you're going to be conditioned to add a bit of friction into your life so you feel the exhilaration of stretching and improving. You're going to be reminded of times when you did things you didn't think you could do, and then you're going to be inspired to go and stretch again. You're going to feel that rush of energy that comes from growing, struggling and overcoming.

Tomorrow you're going to be better than you are today. And you're going to like yourself more. You're going to feel that boost of self-confidence that comes from improvement.

This is an awesome skill. I love the skill of IMPROVING DAILY.

IT'S IN THE STRIVING

So here's an interesting thought for you—happiness comes in the striving, not in the attaining.

Think about your experiences with this. Remember when you worked really hard chasing a dream, pushing for a victory, or saving for a material possession? Remember how you felt more alive as you got close, but upon achieving the exhilaration soon faded? Then you were on to the next dream, milestone, or possession hoping that *it* would somehow produce your elusive lasting happiness.

We expect the finish line to hold more joy than it does. What we don't expect—which is where we'll actually find it—is that happiness can be obtained every day along the journey.

Recognizing where you're at and how far you've come, focusing on progress and not perfection, and relishing the satisfaction that comes from hard work. That's where exhilaration comes from.

You want to be more alive? You want to feel more awake? It's in the striving.

Enjoying, savoring, and appreciating are all skills that produce happiness. You've been experiencing these along the way. Now you can add "striving" to your bag of skill sets and you've really got something.

— ACTIVITY —

Let's start off with something simple. Take a walk. Walk around the block and see if you can meet someone new. Deliberately seek to introduce yourself to someone you don't already know.

Not only do I want you to meet them and say, "Hi," I want you to get their name and come back and write at least two lines about why you think they're a great person. Train yourself to see the best in people—even people you've barely met.

CHALLENGE YOURSELF

We just shared together about how exhilaration comes in the striving. Now think about what's the opposite. What is counter to stretching, growing, and reaching? What would you say?

Stagnation is the word that comes to my mind. It's feeling mired down. Feeling droopy. It's that state of being asleep or unconscious. Death is another word that seems to be opposite.

Sometimes we get caught up in the misguided thought that happiness is about living on "Easy Street". Or that sitting around doing nothing is "living the good life". But when we realize these lifestyles run parallel with feeling asleep or being sedated, why would we choose that when we can instead choose energy, excitement, and passion, where we can be awake and alive?

The trick is we're repeatedly lulled into sleepy lifestyles of comfort and ease. We're conditioned to take the path of least resistance.

But comfort kills productivity, creativity, and growth. Choose to get outside your safety zone. Start a new hobby. Learn a new language. Visit unfamiliar places. Meet new people and increase your vulnerability.

These are all things you can do to intentionally add a bit of friction in your life. That's where this skill is super important. Yes, problems and misfortunes will challenge us, but allowing only those obstacles to build and shape us is waaay to reactionary. It's not directing and shaping our lives.

Decide where you're going. Decide who you'd like to be and what character traits you'd like to possess, then deliberately, intentionally add your own challenges to your life.

Think of tasks you avoid. Is it out of fear? Tackle them intentionally. Don't be someone ruled by and controlled by fear. Build your self-confidence. Increase your capacities.

Do you feel you're too busy? Yes, we are all busy—but sometimes we use it as an excuse to stay inside our comfort zone of hectic familiarity. It's become our chosen lifestyle.

Changes to your routine don't have to be dramatic—risks can be small and still be effective. Introducing controlled anxiety is like mental cross training. Along with keeping your brain active, it may help you manage the unexpected, out-of-control stuff that's part of life.

I told you about Gregory Berns before. He's the author of *Iconoclast: A Neuroscientist Reveals How to Think Differently*. He writes about how to activate your brain more fully by introducing controlled friction. He says that our brain gains "New insights from people and new environments—any circumstance in which the brain has a hard time predicting what will come next."

Deliberately adding opportunities for unpredictability will help you stimulate brain activity and, thus, more energy in your life.

This doesn't have to be a huge shift in order for it to be effective. Stimulate your brain by introducing challenges. Crossword puzzles, chess, riddles, and other mind games can keep you sharp and active.

Boost your creativity by experimenting with new combinations or by doing free-association exercises. You can even gamify routine activities to add spice to your life—you know, maybe you decide to brush your teeth with your non-dominant hand, or do household chores with your eyes closed, or maybe cook without a recipe, simple exercises that add a bit of spice to life.

Now, if you want to raise the stakes, do activities that introduce an audience element such as practicing public speaking skills, performing in community theater, or reading to elementary school children.

These are just ideas to get you thinking. The point is, if you only let your daily setbacks and normal adversity shape your personal development, you are missing out on awesome opportunities to deliberately shape and mold your life.

Push yourself to do and be more. They say, "The limit is not the sky. The limit is in the mind."

– ACTIVITY –

Today, I want you to go TV-free all day. But this isn't just about taking away time wasters; I want you to find more constructive things to do with your time. Get out of the house. Enjoy a hobby. Read. Serve. Build. Live.

Then, of course, come back and write about your experience in your journal.

LIVE WITH INTENTION

A popular saying is, "Live with intention, not out of habit."

It's easy to fall into a routine. We create routines so our brains don't have to process continually. They help us be consistent and efficient. We survive with routines, but break them and we thrive.

According to the Yerkes-Dodson Law[30] (this was discovered back in 1908 and it still holds true), when we're in a state of relative comfort we can achieve only a steady level of performance.

Introducing anxiety improves our performance levels at a greater rate. Too much anxiety and we freeze up and get stressed out; however, if we attain "Optimal Anxiety," we improve dramatically.

Do things that cause you to grow. Stretch yourself through intentional unfamiliarity. Break your routine. Introduce risk. Change your perspective. The key is to take charge of your personal development. Choose to live with a purpose.

So how do you do that? Here are some ideas:

First off, start a journaling habit. Journaling is one of the activities proven most effective in receiving the satisfying benefits found through positive psychology. Taking time to stop and consider, to recognize and reflect, and then to evaluate and articulate will bring focus and clarity to your thinking.

By writing our thoughts down we create opportunities to express gratitude and appreciation and gain insights into our thoughts we otherwise might have overlooked.

There are many types of journals you can keep as well as reasons to keep them. You can create a gratitude journal for yourself by writing three to five lines each day, or you can create a thoughtful "handbook for life", designed to share some of the things you've discovered in life, or a "words of wisdom" anthology, or a collection of your "life observations" that you can pass down to your children as heirloom-quality insight books.

Another idea is to do a 30-day challenge. Have you ever participated in a 30-day challenge? Have you ever been the instigator?

Think of what you've always wanted to do, or an area in your life where you currently want to grow or improve. Then set yourself a challenge. Maybe you want to see stay sugar-free for 30 days or meditate daily.

You can use a 30-day challenge to limit your social media or TV consumption.

Maybe you want to do a specific exercise regime for 30 days. Or you might want to do a 30-day challenge to rid yourself of negative self-talk or a bad habit of complaining.

Find your goal—something you want to do for you, not for someone else. See how much improvement you can make in that area in just one month. They say nothing of value ever gets done without a deadline. Set it and go.

Remember what Mark Twain said about personal progress. "The secret of getting ahead is getting started."

Why is it that New Year's Resolutions often make us depressed? We set these goals that we super want to attain. Then, since we haven't created a system to help us actually accomplish the resolutions, we drift back into our old ways, and anytime we think of our resolution we feel guilt and shame.

Here are some suggestions that might help.

First, create and save your to-do lists. Check off what you've accomplished each day, and save the lists in a shoebox or a jar—somewhere visible.

Another effective happiness boost is to hold an end-of-the-year review party to remind yourself of all your accomplishments. We do this in our home. We keep a clear, plastic box in the kitchen where we can write down our personal triumphs. Or maybe it's something awesome that one of the kids has done. We do this regularly. Then, at the end of the year, we have a family party and pass around all the cards with the triumphs and successes. It makes for a very positive celebration.

— ACTIVITY —

Today I want you to eat only when you're hungry. Challenge yourself to live with intention today. Don't hit that 3pm snack break simply because that's what you always do. Break your normal routines and eating habits by eating only when you're hungry (and, no, you're not hungry all the time).

Feel empowered as you realize you're in charge—you're not
controlled by your stomach or bad habits.

FIND YOUR MOTIVATION

Determine your motivating force—find the reason why you do things. Is it out of fear? Habit? Obligation? Do you feel you're being forced or coerced to do it? Or are you driven to do it out of passion or because it touches the deepest level of your being?

We receive far greater personal rewards when they're intrinsically motivated. Without even changing what you're doing you can alter why you're doing it. For example, you can grudgingly attend a dinner with your in-laws because your spouse is making you, or you can choose to go because you find great pleasure in seeing your spouse smile or because you enjoy the challenge of eluding their conversational traps about your career.

When you make the choice to bring your motivational force inside, you control your happiness payoff.

Your biggest payoff will be if you determine your big why. Viktor Frankl spoke often about this is his book, *Man's Search for Meaning.* Having a mission, a purpose, a calling makes all the difference.

We talked about this at the end of SKILL #3 where you chart a course for a meaningful life and you go through some exercises to figure out where your passions lie.

Have you figured out your purpose or a calling in life? Do you have something to contribute that nobody else can offer?

Ask yourself this question: If you were free to do anything in the world, what would it be? Say you won the lottery—$50 million dollars. What would you do first? Sure, you'd take a vacation. Ditch the tie. Possibly the job. Indulge in some costly products for a while. But then what? After a while you'd get bored. Every day would be just like the last. Looks like money wasn't what you were after all along, so what is it?

To keep from being bored you're going to have to figure out what you are going to do with all your time, your energy, and your money. What are you going to do that you feel will be significant? Answer that question and you may have found your calling or purpose in life.

And if you've already found your purpose, figure out how to accomplish it even though you haven't yet won the lottery. Do this and you're on the fast track to enjoying a meaningful life.

Fabienne Fredrickson said, "The things you are passionate about are not random. They are your calling."

— ACTIVITY —

Enjoy your own self-proclaimed Day of Kindness. Pick a day then challenge yourself to be overly kind to others. Smile at strangers. Extend compassion to those you may have thought undeserving. Go out of your way to help around the office or at home. No one need know about your secret holiday or your personal motivation.

Then come back and write about your experience in your journal.

ENVISION YOUR FUTURE SELF

What are you going to be like in five, ten, or twenty-five years? Well, what would you *like* to be like?

In *The Alchemist*, Paulo Coelho said, "It's the possibility of having a dream come true that makes life interesting." Why not have a dream? Why not pursue your goals?

Envision what your life will be like when those dreams come true. Now write them down. List out what your daily routines would be like, what you'd do with your spare time, what contributions you'd make to those around you, and how you'd treat others who have not been quite as fortunate.

Remember what we talked about with visualizing your life? Films aren't created without some serious visualization, why would your dreams be any different?

So take some time and really visualize out what you'd like your life to be like. Spend enough time visualizing it out that you can see it, feel it, smell it, and even taste it. I know a man who visualized his dream house out so well that he could smell the aroma in his home office. Now everyone who comes to visit his beautiful office comments on the calming scent.

To help you get in this mindset, write a letter to your future self. Create your own personal time capsule. Envision what you'd like your life to be like. Imagining you're older, what would you like to be doing? What kind of relationships are you looking for? What have you found to be most important? What contributions will you have made?

Now write to yourself about today. Tell Future You what you've decoded to change today to ensure the better future. Tell Future You about your goals and why you've set them. Talk to yourself about sacrifice and how you're giving up momentary pleasures or indulgences in hopes that Future Self will accept and appreciate the gift. Seal it and tuck it away with a note on when you can open it. Note: You can use a service like FutureMe.org to send yourself an e-mail in the future.

Now let's make a personal development plan.

Someone wisely counseled, "You can't plow a field by turning it over in your mind." You've got to put things into action. What are the goals you'd like to achieve? List them out and write them down. They say a plan is a dream with a deadline. Don't let it just be a dream.

Now list smaller goals that will put you on the road to achieving those larger goals. What needs to be done today, tomorrow, or within the month? Create milestones and write them down.

Once you have a series of milestones, you can further break those down by listing out specific tasks you can do each day to get you closer to each milestone and each end goal.

I'd like to pass on Jack London's counsel here. He said, "You can't wait for inspiration. You have to go after it with a club."

With your personal development plan you should also have your own personal mission statement.

Successful companies have them. When they're properly defined, well articulated, and align with the true purpose of the business, they can be powerful tools in unifying all company efforts to achieving the common goal. It's a reminder to stay focused—"Remember, *this* is what we're all about." Well, what about you? What's your purpose? What do you want your contribution in life to be?

Take the time to ponder what your values are. What your "unique voice" is. What is your true essence? Your distinctive DNA? Your passion? Then state what impact you expect to have on the world. It will take some time to develop this. Write it down then reflect on it frequently, making adjustments and refinements as necessary.

– ACTIVITY –

Today's lesson is the activity. Take time to write your own personal development plan and your personal mission statement. Don't worry, it doesn't need to come out all polished and perfect the first time. This document is a work in progress, but you will need to start it in order to see any progress.

Write your personal development plan and mission statement down below, but also keep a copy on your smartphone so you can regularly review and update it.

AVOID STAGNATION

Albert Einstein said, "Life is like riding a bicycle. To keep your balance, you must keep moving."

Maybe you're feeling sluggish like you just don't have enough energy for daily life. Or maybe you've reached a plateau and you're not sure now to take yourself to the next level. Stopping or coasting are *not* the answers. Look at nature. When water stops flowing it becomes stagnant and a prime breeding ground for bacteria and diseases. Rushing water, on the other hand, is full of vitality and actively nourishes everything around.

Find ways to keep yourself from stagnating. Make your own personal development plan. Learn new skills (in your field or out). Engage in new hobbies or activities. Plan ways to grow socially, emotionally, physically, spiritually, or intellectually.

Ask yourself if what you are doing today is getting you closer to where you want to be tomorrow.

One effective way to avoid stagnation is to create an exercise program that sticks. We all know the physical benefits we will get with a regular exercise program—increased strength, stamina, weight loss and a stronger immune system. But did you know it also does wonders for our mental well-being?

Research shows exercise can also help reduce stress, boost endorphin levels (our bodies' chemicals that make us feel happy), increase creativity, improve self-confidence, enhance productivity, and alleviate anxiety.

So what's stopping us? Oh, yeah, we are. We forget; we procrastinate too much; or we lack the motivation necessary to make it an effective routine.

If you've learned anything through the course of this book, you've probably learned that you have the power to spark seismic change in yourself just by making conscious, deliberate choices.

Put your mental powers to good use. Use mindfulness techniques to develop and carry out an effective exercise program. Here are a few tips to make a regular exercise program part of your routine:

- Exercise with friends—using the buddy system will keep you motivated, consistent, and strengthen relationships at the same time
- Change it up—do a variety of physical activities to keep things fresh and fun
- Pick a specific time—first thing in the morning is effective for making your routine automatic
- Chart your progress—whatever you chart improves. There are tons of apps and gadgets to help you track consistency, monitor progress, and set goals

- Don't just focus on weight loss—remember it's all about the journey, not the end goal

Use the mindfulness skills you've learned in the 7 Core Skills of Everyday Happiness to improve your overall physical well-being. Remember, flourishing is about achieving success in *every* aspect of life. You're more likely to achieve this state when you're happy, which, of course, you have the power to spark.

One important thing to know is that consistent exercise can do wonders for your self-esteem too. It comes down to the power of integrity.

I look at integrity as doing what you say you're going to do. Simple as that. Here's a story.

I met a man who is the CEO of a media company, a wildly successful man who is prosperous in more ways than mere money. He's confident, athletic, insightful and well balanced. As we talked, he told me he wasn't always like that.

He said growing up he lived in the shadow of his father. He yearned for (unsuccessfully actually) the approval and admiration of his dad.

And it destroyed him. Well, for a long time anyway.

Growing up, he had low self-esteem. He felt that, since his dad didn't love him, he was unlovable to everyone else. His confidence was shot. Life was harder than it had to be.

Then he told me the secret to his turnaround. He said he decided to be completely honest and true to himself.

It started with exercise. He made a plan to exercise three times a week. He wasn't doing this for anyone else. He was doing it for himself. And he held himself accountable. Every time he was true to his word—every time he exercised when he told himself he was going to—his confidence grew.

He began to expand on his self-promises. He set standards for himself with his eating patterns, with his personal interactions, and with his study habits. As he kept his promises to himself, not only did his self-confidence shoot through the roof, but he also improved mentally, socially, spiritually, physically, and, of course, economically.

This model CEO is what I expect true success is—where you thrive in *all* aspects of your life.

I find it awesome that it all started with integrity. It started with him being absolutely true to his word. Being true to himself.

— ACTIVITY —

Today, gamify your normal routine. Pick the aspect of your routine you want to change up and decide how. It could be brushing your teeth or doing your chores with your non-dominant hand. It could be taking a new route to work and seeing how many street signs you can memorize.

You pick the routine and you pick the game. Tonight, write about your experience.

BUILD MOMENTUM

Pablo Picasso said, "Inspiration exists, but it has to find you working." Good wisdom.

OK, so we've got some big, hairy audacious goals (BHAGs as coined by Jim Collins in his book, *Built to Last: Successful Habits of Visionary Companies*). How do we keep ourselves from getting burned out or discouraged? I mean the gap between where we're at and where we want to be is huge.

The secret lies in the pacing.

Do something every day that gets you closer to where you want to be. It doesn't have to be huge. Just a step. Now stick to it. Be consistent. You can make it a morning routine, set an alarm to remind you at a certain time each day, keep a journal noting each day's efforts, or employ friends and family as a support group.

Understand the length of the journey. You're in this for the long haul. Take time regularly to track your progress. One idea is to map out how far you've come and what you've experienced. Just as you'd use a paper map to chart a physical journey, create a visual map so you can see—actually see—how far you've travelled. Review this often, and note your significant milestones and progress—your increased strength, stamina, and understanding.

Reward your improvements. Like monetary interest, daily effort compounds.

Brad Gast says, "Have an unrelenting belief that things will work out, that the long road has a purpose, that the things you desire may not happen today, but they will happen. Continue to persist and persevere."

Another super effective technique is to build a support system. Get people on your team.

So here you are. You've got a firm idea of what you want to accomplish. You've detailed out the steps that will help you get there and you've identified daily tasks that will bring you closer. The next think you'll want to do is create an accountability and support system.

There are many ways you can achieve this. You can enlist friends who know what you want to accomplish and who will serve as your support group or you can hire an accountability coach. This is an effective route that highly successful people choose. I mean what high performing athlete or musical performer doesn't have a coach or advisor?

A third option is to join a Mastermind group with like-minded people.

Just because it's a "personal" development plan doesn't mean you have to do it all by your lonesome. Get a friend, a team, or a coach to encourage you all along the way. Together we're always more.

Lastly, don't quit. Always keep improving. Always keep striving.

The legendary cellist Pablo Casals was asked why he continued to practice at age 90. He replied, "Because I think I'm making progress."

— ACTIVITY —

Make a list of three things you want to accomplish in the next six months. Then, under each of the three things, I want you to write down two things that will need to be done in the next month to accomplish that six-month goal.

Wait ... you're not done. For both of those two things that need to be done this month, I want you to write two more things that if you did them this week would put you right on track for accomplishing your monthly goal.

Write them in your journal, but also keep a copy of this on your smartphone.

"And suddenly you know: It's time to start something new and trust the magic of beginnings."
— *Meister Eckhart*

CHAPTER 12
SKILL #7 – BEGIN AGAIN

OH, YEAH! YOU'VE MADE IT TO THE FINAL CHAPTER—the final skill of the 7 Core Skills of Everyday Happiness.

You've done amazing stuff. Look how far you've come! You've learned about the Three Mindsets of Success, and you've changed some of your limiting beliefs. You're feeling your soul expand as you realize you are powerful; you are capable of much, much more.

You've learned that it absolutely matters what we focus on. You've learned you can stop obsessing over everything you feel you're missing in life, and instead feel happiness now by choosing to deliberately, consciously focus on what is going right in your life.

You've learned about the Skill of Gratitude, how it's the king of all the other skills of happiness. You've found that you can't be truly grateful and unhappy at the same time. So now that you know this … now that you've worked on the Skill of Gratitude … you realize happiness is actually a choice. Whenever you want to spark up your happiness levels, you simply need to actively focus on things you're truly grateful for.

Don't forget that a big part of gratitude is remembering you are the recipient of deliberate kindness. People care about you.

You learned how to SAVOR THE NOW—how to make all the good stuff in life last as long as humanly possible. You learned how to be truly present and techniques for how to enjoy the present as the gift it is. You've learned to remove distractions and to live deliberately.

You were reminded about the value of service, of lifting someone else. You also practiced this as you engaged in the various activities. Remember, service is one of the skills that too frequently gets forgotten. And also remember the Yagottawanna principle—how you can bring your motivations internal and enjoy the full benefit of premeditated compassion.

You've been empowered with how to remove stress, anxiety and worry from your life. You've learned how to rewrite the horrible, terrible, tragic stories you've been telling yourself—you know the hypothetical ones with the horrific endings of something that might-could-maybe-possibly happen.

On the flip side, you've found that anger is a choice and that complaining reveals a negative, completely ungrateful heart. You've found how you can reverse these and turn negatives into positives.

You were reminded of the value of positive relationships—that you can't be truly successful without the kind of deep personal connections we crave. Hopefully, you've made efforts to forgive others and to repair relationships.

You have been energized with the idea to IMPROVE DAILY by deliberately adding controlled friction to your life, inviting "optimal anxiety" in as a way to fuel growth. And you've made a personal development plan and a mission statement. Hopefully, you made great strides toward finding out what your purpose in life is—what it is that only you can accomplish. Finding this and then striving every day to fulfill it will bring such lasting happiness.

And now you're here. You're DONE. FINISHED. Your personal development is OVER.

Of course, we both know that's not true. Yes, in the movies we get to this climactic conclusion where our hero has been striving, striving, striving against these seemingly insurmountable odds ... only to come up against the biggest, baddest, most challenging obstacle ever.

No one would fault our hero for giving up, for quitting. The challenge is that huge. But still we hope for our hero. We cheer and encourage the hero on. And when that final challenge is surmounted there's exhilaration…

and…

then…

it's…

over.…

There's nothing more to watch really.

The challenges have been surmounted. The battle has been won. So we leave the theater. We move on to find another story, one with a new challenge, with a new hero—and new inspiration for our own lives.

We crave the journey.

Welcome to the chapter on Skill #7: BEGIN AGAIN where you will learn to intentionally, deliberately start over, add variety, take a fresh approach, renew, revive, and rekindle in order to keep striving and have the zest and excitement in life that is always available for you—if you choose it.

Welcome to Skill #7: BEGIN AGAIN.

YOU FAILED. GOOD. HERE'S WHY

Today's lesson is called, "You failed. Good. Here's why." I like that. It makes me smile. Mostly because I've "failed" so many times—and so many times it totally demoralized me. Now that I can see "failure" in the proper light, I realize it's all been a wonderful training ground for the wild success I'm achieving today.

Trust me. You'll love today's lesson.

Listen to successful people brag. Do they boast about how easy it was? How it was simply handed to them or how they barely had to put forth the effort? No, they boast about how hard it was, how they failed, and failed, and failed again. But then—and here's where people lean in as they tell their story—they went at it one more time with every ounce of conviction, every shred of determination, every spark of courage they could muster from the deepest reaches of their soul, and that's when they succeeded. And boy did they succeed.

Failure is a stepping-stone to eventual success. It's the motivating force in an action movie that propels our hero forward. Think about any action movie that you love. Does the hero succeed at first? No. NEVER. It's attempt ... after attempt ... after attempt. We continue watching because we love their unconquerable spirit. We cheer them on because they're going against seemingly impossible odds. We *want* them to win. To succeed. To triumph.

Repeated failures make for much more compelling stories. So if you've failed, you're on the path trod by Life's most honored and successful people. Follow them implicitly. Do what they did and pick yourself up and go at it again.

I love this quote by Winston Churchill. He said, "Success is going from failure to failure with no loss of enthusiasm." To which Truman Capote added, "Failure is the condiment that gives success its flavor."

Now here's another concept you may wish to soak in.

You don't have to have it all figured out to move forward. Sometimes you just need to ... move forward.

Take the lessons learned from "The Marshmallow Challenge[31]". Teams are given 20 sticks of spaghetti, one yard of tape, one yard of string, and one marshmallow, which must be on top. They're then challenged to create the tallest freestanding structure in the allotted time.

This experiment has been replicated many times with consistent results—kids generally do better than business school students. Why? They spend more time playing and prototyping. When it doesn't work, they go at it again. Business school students are too smart for that. They spend most of their time analyzing, discussing, and planning. Then, when their plans fail, they spend the rest of their time fixing it, determined to make their plans work. The kids? They just have fun attempting, learning, adjusting, and rapidly testing new ideas.

To inspire you to move forward, I share this quote by Arianna Huffington. "Failure is not the opposite of success, it's part of success."

Trust the magic of new beginnings. Make the magic. Live deliberately.

– ACTIVITY –

Whether you realize it or not, you may be struggling to get over a prior failure. Today, do this exercise: Go to Wikipedia and read about someone who repeatedly failed then turned that into amazing success. Possible candidates could be: Walt Disney (multiple early business failures), Steve Jobs (fired from the company he helped start), Colonel Sanders (his new recipe was rejected 1,009 times), Henry Ford (broke five times), or Oprah Winfrey (demoted and told she "Wasn't fit for television").

So many people have experienced wild success after numerous failures. Mimic their persistence. I love this quote by Thomas Edison. "I have not failed; I've just found 10,000 ways that won't work."

Read about a heroic successful person who failed repeatedly then open up your journal and write what has inspired you about their story.

DO THE REBOOT

Here's a simple concept for you today. Do the reboot. You do it to your computer or mobile device when you feel it's running sluggish. Hollywood does it to a movie or television series to breathe new life in. Organizations do it too. Rebooting is the process of intentionally starting over.

It's purposefully initiating a fresh start designed to discard what's in the storage memory area so you can BEGIN AGAIN without the weight of excess baggage.

How can you apply this concept to your life? Are there things in your collected memory that are holding you back? That put undue focus on a storyline that isn't in alignment with where you're headed? Or that limit future growth and development?

Do a reboot. Take cues from Hollywood. Keep the main characters, but forget the backstory and start over. Today is a brand new day—allow it to be such.

One important thing to clear from your memory when you do the reboot is to get rid of any limiting beliefs. These are statements you tell yourself that hold you back. You know, when you say, "I'm not good enough, or smart enough, or I'm not a writer, or I can't play sports like so-and-so, or I'm not a social person, or I'll never … whatever."

These are limiting beliefs that need to go.

We've talked about these limiting beliefs before. You may wish to review the 3 Mindsets of Success video series. You can find a link to them at nCOURAGE.LIFE. It is so important to recognize when we're slipping into a limited mindset and then take the steps to move into a growth mindset and eventually a deliberate mindset.

So, today, do the reboot. Take a quick walk around the building. Then, when you come back in, boot up. You're totally new.

— ACTIVITY —

Today, forgive yourself. Consider a mental burden you've been carrying around. Maybe it was a mistake or a failure. Choose to forgive yourself. Consider the lesson you gained. Appreciate it. Then move on. Think of your mistakes as stepping-stones to somewhere higher.

In your journal write what you've forgiven yourself for and how you're going to move forward.

LEARN TO UNLEARN

Sometimes we feel we can't do something. We feel trapped or victimized by our circumstances. In these cases, we have falsely conditioned ourselves into a state of "learned helplessness".

In the *Star Wars* movie, *The Empire Strikes Back*, the great Jedi master, Yoda, instructs a young apprentice who is mired in negative, I-can't-do-it-thinking. In this valuable lesson, he says simply, "You must unlearn what you have learned."

Martin Seligman, the father of positive psychology, discovered "learned helplessness" is a condition when, because of previous negative experiences, people feel they have no control to avoid unfavorable situations so they give up and don't even try. Those experiencing symptoms of depression often exhibit high levels of learned helplessness.

Don't fall victim to this way of thinking. An avalanche of positive psychology research shows that simply by believing in positive outcomes we can effect profound personal change.

You are not the victim of your environment; in fact, by making deliberate, conscious choices—you're the creator.

Learn to unlearn. Allow new possibilities to enter your brain. Get rid of negative phrases such as, "I can't," or, "I'll never," or, "I'll always..." Purge yourself from limiting beliefs. Expect good things to happen. Introduce controlled friction into your life, deliberately engaging in activities that stretch or scare you.

Maya Angelou said, "You may encounter many defeats, but you must not be defeated. In fact, it may be necessary to encounter the defeats, so you can know who you are, what you can rise from, how you can still come out of it."

Let's reprogram your predictive coding.

You've likely already experienced predictive coding when you've typed something into your computer browser and it automatically suggested what it thought you were looking for.

In the psychology world, predictive coding is where you imagine scenarios you expect to happen and they do—whether fortunate or not. Opportunistic or pessimistic self-fulfilling prophecies fall into this category.

The good news is you can apply positive psychology principles to visualize favorable scenarios you'd like to see fulfilled. Then your mind will be coded to recognize the patterns and signals of your desired outcome. For example, if you've been doing the exercise of writing down three fortunate things each day that happen to you then you have been conditioning your mind to look for the repeated patterns of deliberate goodness in your life.

Opportunity knocks and you're listening. Practice exercises in the BE GRATEFUL and SAVOR THE NOW skill sets to train your brain to pick up on the positive trends currently in your favor.

— ACTIVITY —

Today, expect something wonderful is going to happen. Don't just hope for it—expect it. To make this come about easier, strive today to find the good in everything—problems, opportunities, challenges, relationships, your commute . . . everything. Consider that today the Universe is conspiring to teach you, train you, or bring you something wonderful.

COURT HER AGAIN

Remember how your relationship was when it was brand new? There was excitement mixed with a heavy dose of uncertainty. Did she like you? For that matter, did she even notice you? You obsessed not only about *asking* these kinds of questions but also on *intervening* enough to ensure the answer was a resounding, "Yes!"

Your courtship was focused purely on making her happy. You thought more about what she liked and disliked. You were patient. Available. Willing. And you were rewarded. There was energy and excitement—that special spark that made your relationship magical.

Well, why not court her again? Put in the same amount of energy as you did before. Remove your distractions. Make those sacrifices. Strengthen your friendship. Nurture your relationship. Win her heart. You've already proven you are a winner. Sweep her off her feet again.

Now, I just said this all from the guy's perspective; please don't be offended, ladies. You absolutely can put in the same effort to rekindle your relationship;

this is not a one-way street. Remember all the research we've shared about how our minds get bored if we are in a state of ease, familiarity, or predictability?

The point is plateaus are natural, routines invite boredom. It's easy for relationships to go stale or for monotony to set in, but—and I've got to be frank here—that's really dumb if we *allow* this to happen to our relationships and to our lives. Live with zest. Love with a purpose. Keep things fresh and alive in your life. Gardens need weeding. Walls sometimes need to be repainted. Why would we allow our best sources for happiness—our relationships—to get stale, mundane, or dull?

If you've learned *anything* from this book, I hope you've learned that you *absolutely* have the power to change your circumstances. You are the creator of the quality and exhilaration of your life.

When I say BEGIN AGAIN it doesn't suggest throwing away your current relationships and starting over. Again that's dumb, dumb, dumb (sorry for my bluntness). It's about once more putting in the time, energy, and effort into your *current* relationships. BEGIN AGAIN. Deliberately, consciously bring back the energy, care, concern, and unselfish attention to your relationship.

I shared this before and it is absolutely worth repeating. Tony Robbins said, "Do what you did at the beginning of a relationship and there won't be an end."

— ACTIVITY —

Today's activity is PROJECT: REKINDLE

Want to rekindle the spark you had early on in your relationship? Put this exercise into practice. Deliberately, intentionally set out to rekindle your relationship. Here are some suggestions: Plan five things you can do each week to show you care. Make a list of the possibilities. Recreate your first date. Write a love letter. Plan a double date. Do extra chores around the house. Discover and speak your spouse's "love language". Give uninterrupted attention. Do the things he/she loves to do. Meet him/her at the door when coming home from work. Make an "I remember when" memory book. Go down "memory lane" to meaningful locations you've shared. With PROJECT: REKINDLE, make focused efforts to improve communication lines and appreciation levels.

One important note: Don't use the skills you've been learning in this series as a way to manipulate or attempt to shape someone else's behavior. These skills are to teach you how to adjust your own personal mindset and not to exert undue control over someone else. Striving to rekindle relationships starts with rekindling how you feel.

There are patterns of laziness you've drifted into through the years (don't worry, we all do it). Your opportunity is to change your mindset and enjoy how circumstances change. Even if the only thing that changes in your relationship is how you feel about your significant other—that's hugely significant.

Pick how you're going to accomplish PROJECT REKINDLE and write your premeditated plan in your journal.

BEWARE THE ROUTINE

Beware the routine. This is such an important concept to grasp.

Applying the Seven Core Skills of Everyday Happiness will spark new levels of happiness. For example, writing in a gratitude journal will help you learn to recognize and appreciate blessings you already possess. As you start journaling, you will begin training your brain to spot positive connections in common, ordinary occurrences that will activate good feelings and increase your enjoyment levels. This simple exercise will do wonders.

But beware the routine. Setting a goal for yourself to write daily in a gratitude journal may start out as a refreshing idea and end up as a chore if it becomes too routine.

Also, the neuroplasticity nature of our brains will cause us to adapt to the positive emotions, lessening both their intensity and effectiveness.

There's a simple solution. Add variety.

So, with our example, if you're used to writing in a gratitude journal, pivot slightly and use your journal to record personal insights, words of wisdom, or inspiring quotes.

You can also change your journal prompt. Don't just write about three fortunate things that happened to you today, find new stimuli through which to explore your grateful emotions.

Change your perspective. Write from the point of view of your dog or your boss. Altering the time of day that you write can also rekindle the positive effects you once got from journaling.

If you're used to recording your thoughts at the end of the day, set a reminder to yourself to write at 10am or 3pm. You can also pick one day a week to write instead of every day.

Make it a game. There are so many ways you can modify any activity to keep it fresh, meaningful, and effective. If an activity is starting to become boring or routine, it's simply an opportunity for you to level up.

This concept works for any part of your life that is feeling tedious and boring. Change your routine … change the predictable nature to allow new connections and possibilities.

Live with a deliberate mindset.

– ACTIVITY –

Do something totally new today. Find something risky enough to put butterflies in your stomach. Be fearless. Go after things that scare you. Challenge yourself and today take a calculated risk.

Pick the activity today. Then write about it in your journal.

MAKE IT A ROUTINE

Another suggestion for enjoying everyday happiness is to make it a routine.

Whoa. Whoa. Whoa. I know what you're thinking. *You just said that routines were bad. Now you're completely contradicting yourself.*

True, routines can produce negative effects when they introduce boredom and complacency. But some routines enable us to operate without even thinking, which you can use to your advantage if you set them up that way.

Routines can help us operate throughout the day without engaging any of the decision-making functions of our brain. These are better known as "habits". Of course, they can be positive or negative. Some negative habits are frustrating and can be hard to break. Positive habits, on the other hand, like brushing your teeth, riding a bike, even parallel parking, help us get daily chores done while we're basically on autopilot.

Where developing positive habits can be most helpful for you is in creating deep-seated positive behavioral reactions—the kind of reactions that will help you employ some of the key happiness skills automatically.

If you create routines that condition your brain to react positively when confronted with challenges (for example, you look for the lesson in every trial), you are providing an automated layer of defense against slipping back into old, negative ways of thinking.

Remember some of our mental triggers and how we could use them to deliberately put ourselves into the mindset we wanted? Remember the coins in the street trigger to get yourself in a mindset of abundance, or the "lightly leashed" elephant story, or eliminating the phrases like "I'll be happy when…"? These are some of the triggers we gave you so you could make a positive mindset a natural, instinctive reaction.

Creating positive routines will help you weather the unforeseen challenges ahead by conditioning your brain to instinctively avoid the ruts and seek for the higher ground.

– ACTIVITY –

Think back to the many mental triggers we've helped empower you with. Some of these are phrases like, "Time to get off the negative thinking train," while others are visuals. Write down the mental triggers that best resonated with you and further commit them to your memory. Have these phrases and images work to help you make choosing a positive, deliberate mindset part of your daily routine.

DO THE NEW

My favorite doctor, Dr. Seuss, said, "Only you can control your future."

When was the last time you did something new, something that felt risky enough to bring butterflies to your stomach?

We're at conflict with ourselves here. On one hand we thirst for the new (that's what the news is all about, or the latest product launch, or the conversation at the water cooler), but on the other hand we relax in the safety of the familiar.

Hmm, thrive vs. survive?

Be adventurous. Go after things that scare you. Challenge yourself. Take calculated risks. Alter your routine with variety—the spice of life. Flourishing is about enjoying the happiest, most meaningful life possible. Ralph Waldo Emerson stated, "The world belongs to the energetic." Enjoy life brimming with vitality.

Let's talk now about how to elude the lapse.

You've been applying the Seven Core Skills of Everyday Happiness and you have transformed your life. You're happier, more fulfilled, and have a purpose to your days. It works! Or, more correctly, *you're* working! Then the inevitable happens. Whether due to slothfulness or a frenzied schedule, you begin slipping back into your old ways. You become reactive, or pessimistic, or you start feeling victimized by your circumstances. You've lapsed into Old You.

Shrug it off; don't let a momentary setback turn into a total relapse. Remember the progress you've made? Remember the control you've had as you've intentionally initiated exercises that have sparked happiness? Find a new set of happiness exercises you want work on then set yourself reminders to put them into action. You've learned you have the power to effect personal change. This is part of the long-term process.

Norman Vincent Peale wisely counseled, "It's always too early to quit."

Here's another visual for you. Something you can use as a mental trigger.

Ever watch young parents as they're encouraging their baby to take their first steps? They cheer them on when they fall, pointing out their accomplishments. *You did two steps! Good job.* Sometimes they pick them up, other times they reassure them they can do it on their own. *You're all right. Let's do it again.*

The falls, the missteps—they're all part of the learning process. So why is it that we beat ourselves up when we fall, or fail, or repeatedly make those aggravating mistakes, lamenting as if it's some horrible fiasco?

As you know, one of the Core Skills of Everyday Happiness is to IMPROVE DAILY. To strive. To stretch. To grow. But how can we improve without risking failure? It's gonna happen, or you're going to get too scared to put forth the effort.

You can do it. But *only* if you convince yourself to be on *your* team. You know what I'm talking about. You've got that inner voice inside. The one you hold those internal conversations with. It's called self-talk, and everyone does it.

The key is successful people practice positive self-talk. They get their inner voice to give them words of encouragement. To lift them up. Cheer them on.

You've seen professional athletes talking to themselves before a big fight, match, or game. They're psyching themselves up. Often they remind themselves who they are, what preparations they've made, and how they're the best.

The great boxer Muhammad Ali was awesome at this. He said, "I am the greatest, I said that even before I knew I was."

Practice positive self-talk. Condition your inner voice to look for and reward the good. Recognizing failure is part of the learning process, but so is picking ourselves up and going at it again.

— ACTIVITY —

Just for today, I want you to condition your inner voice to compliment, encourage, inspire, and motivate you on. One day. That's all we're working on today. One day where all of your inner conversations are positive, where you're on your own team—your own side.

When you're done, come back and write about how your day went with your positive inner voice.

REINVENT YOURSELF

All right! You've made it to the final lesson in this book. Of course, you know this is not really the end. The concept BEGIN AGAIN speaks specifically about this. You've been empowered with all this training. Now you have knowledge—turn that knowledge into wisdom. Wisdom is *applied* knowledge.

Go back through the book and repeat the exercises and review the lessons. You've had an awesome workout at the gym, but you're after a positive mental *lifestyle* and that will take time and repetition. You can do this. Keep up the good work.

So, in our last lesson let's talk about reinventing yourself. This is what you've been doing all along. You've changed from a fixed mindset, a limited mindset, into a growth mindset and eventually you've gotten yourself into a deliberate mindset—likely about many things. You've begun to change, and you're loving how that feels. You feel empowered and you realize there are many, many more opportunities for personal growth out there for you.

You're a new person. Continue to *renew*. Keep yourself fresh and new and exciting. It all starts with your mindset.

Ever notice the tremendous amount of energy that comes from starting something? At the starting line there are questions that will soon be answered, preparation yet to bear fruit, and hopes that may shortly be realized. Your muscles tingle with excitement as you prepare for the starting pistol to fire. Richie Norton, author of *The Power of Starting Something Stupid*, said, "Your life should consist of more than commuting, working, eating, surfing the Internet, sleeping and watching TV. Your life should be filled with purpose-driven experiences and projects that bring excitement, energy, and authentic meaning and joy into your life."

His suggestion is to discover your life's passions, and then pursue them with vigor. Break free from the mundane cycle of life and start your new course even if at first it seems crazy.

An unknown writer said, "Never be afraid to strive for something new. Because life gets boring when you stay within the limits of what you already know."

— ACTIVITY —

Today, I want you to write your own obituary.

Ebenezer Scrooge, in Dickens' famous novella A Christmas Carol, experienced a profound change of heart when face-to-face with his mortality.

Are there things about yourself you'd like to change, improvements that could be made with the help of a little introspection? Do this experiment: Write your own obituary. Obituaries are brief biographies, generally written by a loved one, to announce the recent death of a person. They're news articles chronicling the person's important milestones and achievements. At their core, many speak of why they will be most missed. What would someone write about you?

After completing this exercise, pull an Ebenezer and celebrate the time you have left to make your life count for something. Or, as Mark Twain put it, "Let us endeavor so to live that when we come to die even the undertaker will be sorry."

"It's not the mountain we conquer, but ourselves."
— *Sir Edmund Hillary*

CHAPTER 13

EPILOGUE

NOW THAT YOU'VE GONE THROUGH THIS BOOK, you realize there *is* more life, love, and happiness available to you. And you understand it begins with your mindset—something you absolutely have the power to control.

You've found that small, incremental, sustained progress is the key to building positive habits and eventually turning those habits into a thriving lifestyle wherein you truly flourish in *all* aspects of your life.

You've also found that there are resources and systems designed to help you actually achieve what you've set out to do. Many of these resources can be found at nCOURAGE.LIFE. Log in to access online courses, apps, training videos, documentaries, edutainment films, community support groups, and make coaching connections. These resources are available for individuals as well as groups.

Personal development doesn't have to be a solitary endeavor. Together we are always more.

May you gain the joy and satisfaction that comes with true success—a life filled with love, peace, and purpose.

Sincerely,

Scott Wilhite

ACKNOWLEGEMENTS

I'm a filmmaker by trade. A director. I'm often surprised at the amazing mass of talent that comes together to create an inspiring commercial or a beautiful film. As the director, I'm in the privileged position of having my name attached prominently to the finished piece—to be the public face for work that has taken an entire team of talented people countless hours to produce. I'm often falsely credited for insightful contributions others have made.

I remember one time I was in the kitchen talking with my wife and mentioned this predicament and claimed that I'm not the kind of guy who goes around taking credit for other people's hard work. "Sure you do," she said, "every time you say the words 'my children.'"

We laughed. It's so true. There are so many behind-the-scenes people who make wonderful creations possible. The part they play is absolutely invaluable, yet often invisible to the public eye. They're the unsung heroes of creation.

These few paragraphs of acknowledgements will not come close to thanking all of the extraordinary people who have made contributions in the development and publication of this book. I hope they (as well as those uncredited) find great satisfaction in knowing the part they played has helped many others attain new levels of happiness and fulfillment.

First, I want to thank my friend and brother Ed Colquhoun who inspired me to write this book and create the corresponding online course to teach the skills of happiness. He believed in me waaaay more than I believed in myself and saw the potential this could have in helping others. His dedication and sacrifices to make this possible will not be forgotten. He's a true philanthropist. A visionary. A gift.

To Dr. Christian Laplante who counseled on how small, incremental repeated adjustments make the biggest difference. This methodology is at the heart of the nCOURAGE courses.

I thank the pioneers in positive psychology research and education, the giants upon whose shoulders I now stand: Shawn Achor, Sonja Lyubomirsky, Ed Diener, Martin Seligman and others. Thank you for bringing this amazing research on human potential to life.

To my many mentors—

• Michael McLean, who inspired me to find my voice—the contribution that only I could make.
• David Corbin, who chastised me for failing to unwrap ALL the gifts God has given me and pushed me into public speaking.
• Michelle Young, who taught me how to visualize and design my life in advance the way I would develop a shot list.
• Sandra Fan, who introduced me to the many influencers of CEO Space and the philosophy of cooperation over competition.
• Ron Taylor, who encouraged me time and time again never to give up.

To the many people who have shared their creative talent to move this forward—

• Brian Wilcox, a masterful cinematographer who gave of his time, talents, and camera gear to film the first three nCOURAGE films.
• Collin Hundley and Clay Ellis, the mastermind developers behind the design of the Feed Your Happy app.
• Greg Windley, who provided camera gear to shoot the entire 7 Core Skills course.
• Ken Darrow, who edited this book and cleaned up my tangled mess of freestyle grammar.

I express my gratitude to my mother Nancy who not only believed in me and helped fund both the creation of this book and course, but also lives an exemplary life of hope and optimism.

To my lovely wife, Becca, I wish to express with the deepest gratitude in my heart my appreciation for her love and sacrifices. Striving to create all the materials for this book/course/app/films has been a long, hard journey. If it wasn't for her patience and willingness none of this would even remotely be possible, nor would the journey be worth taking.

Finally, with profound gratitude I thank my Heavenly Father who has blessed me with both challenges and opportunities for growth, who left His fingerprints as he blessed my life with fortunate "coincidences" disguised as tender mercies, and who directed me on this amazing journey to a life of purpose, meaning, and fulfillment.

NOTES

1 https://waynewu.wordpress.com/2009/02/08/learned-helplessness/

2 http://sonjalyubomirsky.com/files/2012/09/Lyubomirsky-Layous-20132.pdf

3 https://www.youtube.com/watch?v=0PoM6LGZiBw

4 http://sonjalyubomirsky.com/files/2012/09/Lyubomirsky-Layous-20132.pdf

5 http://hapacus.com/blog/nuns-prove-happiness-leads-to-longer-lives/

6 http://www.ncbi.nlm.nih.gov/pubmed/690806

7 http://www.forbes.com/sites/susanadams/2012/11/28/why-winning-powerball-wont-make-you-happy/2/#51a33c442b61

8 http://greatergood.berkeley.edu/topic/gratitude/definition

9 https://www.psychologytoday.com/blog/minding-the-body/201111/how-gratitude-helps-you-sleep-night

10 https://www.psychologytoday.com/blog/minding-the-body/201111/how-gratitude-helps-you-sleep-night

11 http://wjh-www.harvard.edu/~dtg/Gilber%20t&%20Ebert%20(DECISIONS%20&%20REVISIONS).pdf

12 http://www.apa.org/research/action/multitask.aspx

13 http://www.health.harvard.edu/blog/astounding-increase-in-antidepressant-use-by-americans-201110203624

14 http://www.forbes.com/sites/susanadams/2014/06/20/most-americans-are-unhappy-at-work/#1cff279e5862

15 http://www.theharrispoll.com/health-and-life/Annual_Happiness_Index_Again_Finds_One-Third_of_Americans_Very_Happy.html

16 http://cdn.volunteermatch.org/www/about/UnitedHealthcare_VolunteerMatch_Do_Good_Live_Well_Study.pdf

17 http://www.tandfonline.com/doi/abs/10.1080/00224540903365554#.
   VOyWl1ZUPKA

18 http://www.amazon.com/Paradox-Generosity-Giving-Receive-Grasping/
   dp/0199394903/ref=sr_1_1?s=books&ie=UTF8&qid=1460047352&sr=1-1&key
   words=the+paradox+of+generosity

19 http://greatergood.berkeley.edu/topic/compassion/definition

20 http://link.springer.com/article/10.1007%2Fs10902-011-9267-5

21 http://www.amazon.com/Why-Good-Things-Happen-People/dp/076792018X/
   ref=sr_1_1?s=books&ie=UTF8&qid=1424808769&sr=1-1&keywords=why+go
   od+things+happen+to+good+people

22 https://www.apa.org/pubs/journals/releases/psp801112.pdf

23 "Something's Coming" by Stephen Sondheim and Leonard Bernstein in West
   Side Story, 1957.

24 http://www.businessinsider.com/minecraft-founder-feels-isolated-
   unhappy-2015-8

25 http://greatergood.berkeley.edu/raising_happiness/post/topic_of_the_month_
   fostering_social_connections/

26 http://www.huffingtonpost.com/entry/cell-phone-hurts-relationships-phone-
   snub_us_560c0cdee4b0dd85030a1c4e

27 https://www.psychologytoday.com/blog/words-can-change-your-brain/201208/
   the-most-dangerous-word-in-the-world

28 https://www.psychologytoday.com/blog/words-can-change-your-brain/201208/
   the-most-dangerous-word-in-the-world

29 http://psychcentral.com/blog/archives/2013/11/30/words-can-change-your-
   brain/

30 http://psychology.about.com/od/yindex/f/yerkes-dodson-law.htm

31 http://marshmallowchallenge.com/Welcome.html

ABOUT THE AUTHOR

Scott Wilhite is an award-winning commercial filmmaker turned social entrepreneur. As a writer, producer, and director he was enjoying a promising creative career without actually enjoying it. During ten of his most productive years he found them to also be ten of his darkest, most unsatisfying years. He felt directionless and that his life was missing purpose and meaning. This all changed when a friend introduced him to the world of positive psychology and showed him the difference that comes from deliberately, consciously choosing what he mentally focuses on.

With his personal transformation, he then created the Feed Your Happy app, produced a three-part video series on The 3 Mindsets of Success, founded nCOURAGE.LIFE, and authored several online mental conditioning courses designed to help people actually put the principles gained in this book into action. *"When I found happiness was a skill, I also found that without continued support it was far too easy to slip back into my old ways of thinking. Tools for deliberate, repeated practice turns a habit of positive thinking into an abundant lifestyle."*

Scott is a husband and father and lives in the Rocky Mountains.

33452314R00117

Made in the USA
San Bernardino, CA
23 April 2019